A Better Way

Faith, Family, and the First Fifty Years of the Opus Group of Companies

Compiled and edited for Gerald A. Rauenhorst, Opus founder,
by William Swanson

FIRST EDITION
Published by the Opus Group of Companies

Copyright©2003
by
the Opus Group of Companies

Design and Production by
Westmorelandflint LLC.
Advertising/Marketing/Public Relations

Library of Congress Control Number
2003114968

International Standard Book Number
ISBN 0-9747195-0-1 OPUS Hard Cover
ISBN 0-9747195-1-X OPUS Soft Cover

Printed in the United States of America
by Bolger Printing, Minneapolis, MN

A Better Way

Faith, Family, and the First Fifty Years of the Opus Group of Companies

Compiled and edited for Gerald A. Rauenhorst,
Opus founder,
by William Swanson

Welcome

Fifty years ago, when I was starting out in business, the idea that someday I'd be reading a book about that business, my family, and myself—if the idea had occurred to me at all—would have seemed preposterous. The notion that fifty years later I'd be helping *tell* that story would have been—well, a long way beyond preposterous.

So you can probably imagine the lingering sense of disbelief with which I greet you at the beginning of these pages. All entrepreneurs are dreamers, of course. They imagine something that's not there yet, and they move toward something on the distant horizon that only they can see. Not accustomed or inclined to look either backward or inward, they leave those jobs to historians and philosophers. Which makes it all the harder to believe that I'm now recounting what my branch of the Rauenhorst family and the Opus Group of Companies we created and run have been up to for the past half century—and how we got here from there.

Well, there's a method to this madness. By talking about the past and present, I like to think my collaborators and I are providing a road map—or a set of guideposts—for the future. In recounting our family and corporate histories, I believe we're laying out a set of personal and corporate principles that will keep both the family and the company strong and successful long after its founder is gone.

You'll notice that I've dedicated the book not only to my wife and partner, Henrietta—Hanky—Rauenhorst, and our seven children, but to future generations as well. I'd love to think that a great-, great-, great-grandchild, or an up-and-coming Opus executive circa 2103—maybe it's one and the same person!—is reading this little volume and saying, "So that's the way it was at the beginning. So that's why we are what we are today!"

At the very least, future readers will learn about some of the major developments of the company's first fifty years—and know the names and contributions of a few of the many wonderful people who have been invaluable to both the family's and the company's success so far. To those individuals who may be reading this hot off the press, on our fiftieth anniversary, I say, Consider this a partial thank you!

"A Better Way"

In his introduction, William Swanson, who compiled, organized, and edited the material that follows, explains the book's design and operation. He left it to me to tell you how we came up with the book's title.

It happened like this:

About ten years ago, Hanky and I were privileged to attend a dinner put on by the Templeton Investment Group in Palm Beach, Florida. As luck would have it, Hanky was seated next to the dinner's featured speaker, Hedrick Smith, the award-winning *New York Times* reporter and author of several highly regarded books on world affairs.

While I chatted with Jane Siebold, who was John Templeton's associate at the time, Hanky and the famous journalist had their own conversation. It turned out that in a remarkably short period of time, Hanky, when asked by Mr. Smith about our background, recounted much of the long history of the Rauenhorst family and the Opus Group of Companies. She told him about the family's hardscrabble beginnings on a Minnesota tenant farm, and how, after my first brief and unhappy experiences working for other people in the construction business, I was frustrated and told her, "There has to be a better way!" She described how I'd set out on my own with a few hundred dollars in borrowed money, built a Lutheran church in my hometown, and established a construction company in the Twin Cities based on honesty, integrity, and hard work. She told him how I'd eventually come to the conclusion that being *only* a construction company wasn't going to satisfy me, convinced as I was as an entrepreneur that there had to be "a better way" to build buildings *and* a company. In business terms, she said, that meant combining design and construction in a pioneering turnkey approach, extending activities to both coasts, and decentralizing corporate operations. As an individual, she concluded, "a better way" meant living a full, rich, and upright life anchored in the core values of faith and family.

Afterward, Mr. Smith told me about Hanky's enthusiastic narrative and said we should write a book. "I even have the title for you," he said helpfully. "You could call it, *There's Got To Be a Better Way.*"

And that, of course, is what we've done, with a slightly streamlined version of Hedrick Smith's suggested title and with a subtitle—*Faith, Family, and the First Fifty Years of the Opus Group of Companies*—that sets out the priorities with which I've tried to live my life.

Now I can only hope that you find the story as interesting as he did.

Gerald A. Rauenhorst
September 2003

To Hanky, our children, and future generations.

CONTENTS

Reflections on a Forty-Year Friendship

By
Monsignor Terrence J. Murphy
Chancellor, University of St. Thomas

The following pages contain scores of memorable stories gleaned from dozens of interviews that reveal the character, life, and activities of Gerald A. Rauenhorst and the Opus Group, the company he founded and built.

It has been a privilege to have hundreds of conversations over the years with this man. Some of them were quick visits over the phone. Others lasted for hours at a time as we walked on a deserted beach or chatted over dinner in his home. Certain themes emerged again and again.

He has a great devotion to his church. He has a deep, all-encompassing love for Henrietta, his college sweetheart and devoted partner for more than fifty-three years, and their unusually close-knit family. He feels a strong sense of fulfillment from an accomplished business career, culminating in this year's fiftieth anniversary of Opus. These core passions of this remarkable man can be summed up in three words: God, family, and Opus. The three words are an apt alternative subtitle for this book.

I have known Gerry and Hanky Rauenhorst for forty years. I consider them to be among my best friends. I vividly remember when our acquaintance began to grow into a deep friendship.

The exact date was May 17, 1966, during a College of St. Thomas event for benefactors, mostly alumni, to announce the departure of Dr. James P. Shannon and my election as president to succeed him—an awesome challenge. After the official announcement, Gerry, with Hanky at his side, walked over and shook my hand. He said, "Congratulations. You have a big job ahead of you." I replied, "I know it, and I'd like you to help. Will you become a trustee of St. Thomas?" He accepted on the spot. It was one of the best decisions of my life. And it began a close relationship that has lasted to this day.

Valuable Lessons

Through the ensuing years I came to know Gerry's brothers and sister. I learned a great deal about his parents, especially his mother, who had an enormous influence on Gerry's life. She taught him valuable lessons that shaped his life and his career.

Gerry grew up in the small town of Olivia, a hundred miles west of the Twin Cities of Minneapolis and St. Paul, during the Great Depression. Life was hard. His parents, who were tenant farmers, had been unable to pay their real estate taxes and lost their farm. That event left a lifelong impression on the small boy. One of Gerry's first childhood memories was of a cold, rainy day in March, when he walked with his parents and siblings to their next farm on a muddy road behind a horsedrawn wagon that carried most of the family's possessions.

Family values and careful attention to detail were indelibly impressed on this young boy. He would grow up to be the founder of the Opus Group, which today has offices around the United States and is one of the foremost real estate developers in the nation.

Gerry's mother insisted that he and the other children study hard in school. She taught them to value education, which she likened to a ladder that one could climb to achieve greater heights. She instilled in Gerry the satisfaction and joy that could come from developing one's potential and improving one's lot in life. Through her, Gerry came to realize the importance of education, not only for the person, but for society and the church.

As a result, Gerry became a leader in Catholic education. He is a trustee of the Papal Foundation. He has received honorary doctorates. He has been a member of the board of trustees of St. Thomas for thirty-seven years, the longest-serving trustee in our history. He was for many years a trustee of Marquette University. With his encouragement, Hanky served on the board of her alma mater, the College of St. Catherine. (He has also served on the boards of several major corporations.)

Gerry's participation in these institutions has not been limited to financial support. The late Father John Raynor, the long-time president of Marquette, where Gerry received his engineering degree, acknowledged the valuable assistance and insightful support Gerry gave him. Gerry faithfully supported Hanky while she was a trustee at St. Catherine's, helping her advise the president. I witnessed firsthand for twenty-five years his intensely personal involvement at St. Thomas. Every major strategic decision at this university during the last almost four decades reflects his wise counsel. Gerry has told me that St. Thomas, which he loves, is never far from his mind.

One of the treasures of my life has been the annual invitation to visit Hanky and Gerry at their home in Florida. Gerry and I have taken long walks on the beach. We have talked about St. Thomas, its present condition, and its future. He has continued that annual tradition with Father Dennis Dease, who succeeded me as president.

Gerry, the visionary, helped me to imagine a campus, especially as we began to develop a downtown Minneapolis presence, that would be more than just a collection of buildings reflecting the fashion of each period and the tastes of different architects and college administrators.

He encouraged St. Thomas to develop a comprehensive campus plan for Minneapolis, an overall "look" that would perpetuate a collegiate style of architecture that had been earlier introduced on our main St. Paul campus. He personally visited Oxford University in England, took pictures, and suggested it as a guide for St. Thomas in Minneapolis. People often comment on the uniform beauty of our campus, particularly its buildings of Collegiate Gothic architecture and Mankato stone, which have become a brand identification for St. Thomas. I give Gerry much of the credit.

And his ideas have not been limited to architecture. They cover the whole life of the university: its intellectual standards, its achievements, its finances, its role in the community, its vision for the future.

Gerry was an early champion of our move to establish that downtown Minneapolis campus. It was his idea to create a grand hall with twelve pillars on which fresco portraits of the major benefactors of the first building are now installed. He repeatedly conferred with his architects and with a gifted artist from Assisi, Italy, to develop a spectacular fresco ceiling depicting the seven traditional Catholic virtues—faith, hope, charity, prudence, justice, temperance, and fortitude.

"Let's have a small, contemporary version of the Sistine Chapel," he said. Fresco painting, which had been an almost lost art in America, was given a new life.

A Determined Man

The counseling at his mother's knee taught Gerry the importance of hard work. Opus today is a reflection of that work ethic. Hanky told me that in the early years of the company, Gerry would often work all night, checking every detail of a project before submitting a bid.

Another lesson he learned from his mother stayed with him throughout life: Make friends carefully and keep them. Friendships he formed in his early years grew over time. I have been amazed at public events in Olivia to see the number of friends of various ages crowd around him. The strong friendships of his early years are still there today.

And always with him is his beloved wife. Clearly, Hanky has been an inspiration, and a solid foundation, for his life's work.

His love for her is evident whenever you see them together. When Gerry was involved in the preparations for his fiftieth class reunion at St. Thomas, Monsignor James Lavin, who works with our alumni groups, asked class members to submit short essays about significant things that happened to them at St. Thomas. Gerry wrote: "In my second year at

St. Thomas I needed a date for Tiger Homecoming, so I called a young lady from Bird Island at St. Catherine's who I barely knew. I have never dated another lady since."

There are two very significant academic programs at St. Thomas that reflect Gerry's interests and values.

One is the study of law. The St. Thomas College of Law had closed for cost reasons during the Great Depression. Every six months or so after he joined our board, Gerry would ask me where my thinking was on reopening the law school. "It must be a law school that emphasizes moral values," he said. On each occasion, I told him I did not feel the time was right, that we simply did not have the funds to start a law school from scratch.

But Gerry is a determined man. I'll never forget a conversation he initiated in the early 1970s. "Father Murphy," he said in his quiet yet forceful way, "if you don't establish a Catholic law school before I die, I will force you to do so by leaving money in my will to establish one." Such was his conviction about the fundamental importance of a faith-based school stressing the moral and ethical underpinnings of the practice of law.

The other academic program is business. I asked Gerry in the mid-1970s for his advice about starting a graduate MBA program. He replied tartly, "I thought we were going to establish a law school. What happened?" I pointed out that St. Thomas already had a very successful under-graduate business curriculum and, at relatively little cost, this could be the foundation of a graduate business education program. I gave him the reasoning of some of our faculty members that a niche existed in the Twin Cities for a part-time night MBA program that would not compete with the very successful full-time day program at the University of Minnesota. He thought about it carefully and then agreed to lead the discussion with our board. But, he said to me, "Let's not forget a law school."

As that graduate business program developed, he became an enthusiastic and generous supporter. It has since grown to be one of the largest MBA programs in the United States.

And the law school? In May 1999, our board voted unanimously to reestablish the University of St. Thomas School of Law. After that momentous meeting, I reminded Gerry about his comment, some twenty-five years earlier, about forcing me to open a faith-based law school. He just looked at me and smiled. Gerald Rauenhorst is not only a determined man; he has a long memory.

Faith and Foresight

Gerry is a man of great faith. His parents taught him that Catholicism is not just a series of teachings, but must play an active role in every aspect of his life. He fervently believes in this principle. As a result, people trust him. They have learned that his private and public lives are grounded firmly in moral convictions. He strongly believes that corporate leaders have an obligation to lead exemplary private *and* public lives. That conviction once caused him to sell his stock in a very promising and ultimately successful company, foregoing millions of dollars in gains, when he learned that the founder and leader of the company was untrustworthy in his private life.

Over the years, while visiting Gerry and Hanky in their home, I've been struck by their love for their seven children. In fact, I know that Gerry's intense involvement in building so many structures in downtown Minneapolis—a development rather late in his career—was due in part to his recognition that many of his children and grandchildren would live and work in the Minneapolis area. He wanted a wholesome business and public environment for them.

Both Gerry and Hanky have told me that their education at St. Thomas and St. Catherine played an important role in helping them shape the values that they have instilled in their offspring. The Rauenhorst children have told me about "Father's college rule." That rule held that they could attend any college they wished, but if they wanted their parents to pay for their education, it would have to be a Catholic school. "And they all did," Gerry says proudly.

When his seven children wanted to show their deep affection, they chose to donate, through their foundation, a chapel at the St. Thomas law school in their parents' honor, a chapel that would offer Mass not only for students, faculty, and staff, but for anyone who works downtown.

The stories are legion about Gerry the quintessential entrepreneur; how he frequently comes up with better ways to do things. I have listened to him as he has described opportunities before they are evident to other people. This ability, combined with his willingness to take prudent risks and the trust that he inspires, are the keys to his business success.

Gerry has demonstrated repeatedly that success begets success. The confidence that people have in him is built on his record of reaching challenging goals. He has profound confidence that he will succeed in whatever he sets out to do. And he usually does.

As I write this, in the summer of 2003, Gerry Rauenhorst is seventy-five years old. I have always marveled that a man who has achieved so much remains the same self-effacing, soft-spoken man I met forty years ago. He says little at St. Thomas board meetings. Others do most of the talking while he listens carefully. But when he does speak, everyone in the room gives him their undivided attention. Once I asked him, "Why don't you speak up more?" He smiled and reminded me of one of his mother's favorite aphorisms: *An empty barrel makes the loudest noise.*

With Gerald Rauenhorst, there is little noise. The barrel is always full.

Introduction

Gerry's Way

By
William Swanson

The first time I encountered Gerry Rauenhorst, I was more impressed by what he *wasn't* than what he was.

What he was, frankly, was something of an enigma, at least to me (and, I presumed, to many of my readers), which is why I went to see him in the first place—and which explains the first sentence of the headline that ran atop the story I wrote about him in the March 1973 issue of *Corporate Report* magazine: *Who Is Gerald Rauenhorst? And Who Says Nice Guys Finish Last?*

What he *wasn't* was your typical entrepreneur cum civic mover-and-shaker circa the early 1970s.

Though I was still young, and relatively new to business journalism, I had already met my share of corporate big shots. More often than not, it seemed, they were physically imposing gents with forceful personalities and booming voices who filled the air with talk of their activities and accomplishments.

Outwardly at least, Gerry was different in almost every way: a five-foot seven-inch, compactly built, soft-spoken, friendly but reserved man who would not be the first, or even second, person you noticed if you walked into a crowded board room.

Like a lot of Twin Citians not readily familiar with the local construction and development business at the time, I was curious about the
large blue hexagonal signs I was seeing along France Avenue and 76th
Street in south suburban Edina. The signs said RAUENHORST, but
the name didn't mean much to most of us. Even the additional words
on the signage—ENGINEERS, CONTRACTORS, DEVELOPERS—
didn't tell a very satisfying story.

When I first asked Gerry about that story, he shrugged and said it was
"just about as typical as they come." To hear him talk, he was just another
small-town kid who, twenty years earlier, had been "trying to make a buck,"
"a typical American boy out to see what he could do in this wonderful
country, accepting the challenge to compete." When I pointed out that
he was, at the relatively youthful age of forty-five, obviously financially
successful, he visibly flinched. "Don't call me a rich man," he said. "I don't
think of it as that." Though he spoke those words softly, I think he was
genuinely put out by the perception.

At that point, twenty years into his business career, Gerry was head-
quartering in a distinctive but hardly overpowering single-story building
on Rauenhorst Circle, along Interstate 494 in Bloomington. The one-man
construction company he had started at his kitchen table, assisted only but
ably by his wife, Hanky, in 1953 had grown to a full-service operation with
250 employees, a steadily increasing number of diverse projects mostly in
the Twin Cities, several large tracts of developable land, and a handful of
subsidiaries.

Then there were his several civic and social involvements, which
included trusteeships at his alma maters, the then College (now University) of St. Thomas in St. Paul and Marquette University in Milwaukee;
leadership roles in several Catholic organizations, including the Knights
of the Holy Sepulchre and the American board of Sogang Jesuit College
in Seoul, Korea; and an innovative, company-sponsored rehabilitation
program for alcoholics called Progress Valley. To that program, the
company was donating one of every forty pretax dollars and one of every
forty executive-group hours.

The Rauenhorst story, in other words, wasn't quite as "typical" as Gerry had wanted me, and *Corporate Report*'s readers, to believe. In fact, by the time I had gotten to know him better, it was clear that Gerry was among the *least* typical entrepreneurs in our part of the world.

I concluded that 1973 article with the following observation:

> Whatever comes in the future, Gerald Rauenhorst is...in a position to talk like a winner. He can say, apparently without the risk of contradiction:
>
> "If this business expands, fine. If it doesn't, well, that's fine too. I really can't say I have any dream, other than to live life to its fullest, accept it as it comes, to accept the challenges."
>
> The point is, he says, there are more important things in life than the Rauenhorst Corporation. It all comes down to a matter of priorities.
>
> "Number one," he says, "is my relation to God and my stand on myself, because I can't do anything for anyone else until I have myself under control." Number two "is my family, and number three is the Rauenhorst Corporation."
>
> Those priorities—spoken without a trace of facetiousness— have held up well over the past twenty years. So well, in fact, that he can also say:
>
> "I wouldn't trade my position with anyone in the world. I'm happy where I am."

"So Far, So Good"

Four years later, when I went back to update the Rauenhorst story for *Corporate Report*, Gerry's position had, quite literally, risen significantly, and he was understandably an even happier man than when I first met him. Which is not to say that he was any taller, louder, or flashier. Gerry, I would come to learn, was simply, uniquely, and consistently Gerry.

He had obviously been, from the very beginning, a man of vision. But by the time of my second visit, that vision was enhanced, again quite literally, by his headquarters' perch on the twenty-third floor of the Northwestern Financial Center, which the company had completed (in a joint venture with the Prudential Insurance Company) in 1974. "Even on a hazy afternoon," I wrote in *CR's* July 1977 feature, Gerry Rauenhorst "can apparently see forever."

His fully integrated design, construction, and development company was finishing its best year ever, with revenues "reportedly" (Gerry wouldn't say for sure) in the neighborhood of $75 million, more than 600 employees, and a geographic reach extending from the Twin Cities eastward to Chicago and west to Arizona. "The firm now owns or controls development of more than 2,000 acres of commercial, industrial, and residential property, and manages well over two-million square feet of office, light industrial, and warehouse space."

Besides all that, on the western horizon almost visible from atop the NFC, was something Gerry called Opus 2—a 440-acre "living-working community" that he was developing in nearby Minnetonka, something quite unlike anything his company, or anyone's company, had built before. Opus 2, about which there will be much more later, was Gerry's corporate masterwork, at least up to that point.

Accordingly, I concluded *that* article with these words:

> "This is my proudest achievement so far," [Rauenhorst] says quickly. "The other things we've done have been pretty much what the marketplace was doing—at least the top edge of the marketplace.
>
> "Opus 2, I think, is unique in the world. Of course, if we had chopped up the land into parcels and sold it as usual, we probably could have made more money, more quickly, than we'll do with Opus 2. But my idea here was to test some innovative ideas.
>
> "So far, we've been lucky. We haven't been proven wrong yet. You never really know until you do something, but so far, so good."

A Constancy of Purpose and Values

As it happened, almost twenty-five years went by before I called on Gerry again. Quent Hietpas, the "semi-retired" senior vice president emeritus at the University of St. Thomas and a longtime friend and confidant of the Rauenhorsts, had called me in the fall of 2001 and asked if I would be interested in helping Gerry write a book. (As a freelance writer, I had already helped Curt Carlson, Earl Bakken, Murray Harpole, and other Twin Cities entrepreneurs tell *their* stories in print.)

My first thought was, "*Gerry?* Write a *book?*"

I remembered, of course, the soft-spoken, self-effacing man who had suffered me kindly if not gladly when I'd asked for his story in the seventies. "So far, so good" was not exactly the tag line of a man dying to share his success saga with the world.

Quent, whom I had known professionally since those long-ago *Corporate Report* days, explained that Gerry was approaching his seventy-fifth birthday, had also "semi-retired" (whatever that means to such relentlessly busy individuals), and wanted to set down the experience of his long and eventful life in a relatively permanent form. More specifically, he wanted to give credit where credit was due, beginning with Hanky and his family, and provide a written record of the first fifty years of the company. Gerry, Quent said, expected the business to last for several generations and wanted future members of the Opus family to understand the values and culture on which the business was built.

That business, by the way, had long since been called Opus Corporation and was now known as the Opus Group of Companies. It had completed more than 2,100 projects around the country, employing more than 1,200 persons nationwide, and was run by chief executive officer Mark Rauenhorst, Gerry's oldest son and second of his seven children. All that I knew, as did much of Gerry's adopted hometown. In 2001, the once somewhat mysterious Rauenhorst/Opus mark was famous throughout the Twin Cities, where the company's projects ranged from St. Thomas' Collegiate Gothic downtown Minneapolis campus to the Best Buy Corporation's enormous new world headquarters in suburban Richfield. So too, despite the family's determinedly low-profile philanthropy, were the fruits of their generosity, which, in Gerry's words, "are dedicated to making the world a better place."

Anyway, just before Thanksgiving 2001, I joined Gerry, Mark, Gerry's eldest daughter, Judy Mahoney (who currently chairs the Rauenhorst family council), and Quent Hietpas at company headquarters, now handsomely set among the hills, ponds, and famous one-way roads of Opus 2 in Minnetonka. The visit was instructive—and, obviously, since you're holding this book in your hands, productive. And, while the setting had changed yet again, Gerry clearly hadn't.

As far as I could tell (and would be able to tell, after many subsequent meetings), Gerry was *still* Gerry. His hair was grayer (whose wasn't?) and he was doctoring a bum shoulder that had effectively shut down his golf game, but otherwise he was to all intents and purposes the same guy who'd first told me his not-so-typical "typical" story back in 1973.

After agreeing to help with his book, I spent time with Gerry at his office in the Twin Cities, at his home in Florida, at the family's lakeside retreat in northern Minnesota, at the spectacular ConAgra world headquarters in Omaha (one of four major Opus-built "campuses" discussed at greater length in Chapter Six), and at various other sites in and around the Twin Cities. What I experienced, besides his easygoing hospitality, was a constancy of purpose and values that hadn't changed at all, as far as I could see, over three decades of remarkable growth, adventure, and achievement.

What's more, over the course of some two dozen interviews with family members, spiritual advisers, college pals, corporate colleagues, employees, and other business people around the country, I discovered that my impressions were apparently shared by everyone who knew anything at all about Gerry.

Successively Better Ways

What follows, then—what grew, in a very real sense, out of those three separate meetings over the course of almost twenty-five years—tells the

Rauenhorst/Opus story as it coincides with Gerry's life to date. It is both a family saga and a corporate history, because it would be impossible to tell one without telling the other. For fifty years, Gerry has not only personified the business he founded, the faith, philosophy, and principles that have guided his personal life have been the company's bedrock as well.

And now a word about how the story is told:

Each of the book's seven chapters describes a key component of Gerry's life, organized in roughly chronological order. The data and commentary that make up each chapter have been derived from interviews (mine and others'—including those conducted by corporate historians Carol Pine and Susan Mundale in 1984 and 1994), family records, corporate documents, speeches, correspondence, press clippings, and sundry other materials, and are presented, in either direct quotation or paraphrased form, as an arrangement of many "voices." The objective is a book that's neither a conventional autobiography, a biography, nor an oral history, but a concert in which Gerry's is the lead voice (it's his story, after all), though by no means the only one. In addition, thirty-six pages of photographs, similarly culled from a wide range of sources, tell the Rauenhorst/Opus story in visual form, also in more or less chronological form.

Gerry has already explained the book's title. While I didn't know it at the time, I realize now that on each occasion I met with Gerry over that quarter of a century, he was showing me successively better ways of doing *something*—of building a building, of growing a company, of raising a family, of living a life.

Which, of course, has been Gerry's way from the beginning.

Chapter One

Beginnings

More than seventy years later, Gerry Rauenhorst could still see the somber tableau in his mind's eye. It was one of his earliest memories—and surely a defining one. And his response, as he remembers it seven decades after the fact, would be typical of his responses to the challenges he'd face the rest of his life.

At the time, he was only four. He was the grandson of a German immigrant, Theodore Rauenhorst, who had come to America in 1846. His father, Henry Theodore Rauenhorst, had made his way to Renville County, in western Minnesota, at the turn of the twentieth century, and with a brother had homesteaded a 240-acre farm between the towns of Bird Island and Olivia. In 1908, Henry had married Margaret Keltgen, a neighbor whose family had immigrated from Luxembourg in the late 1800s, and Henry and Margaret started a family that would eventually number seven boys and a girl.

Henry and Margaret were pious, hard-working, and ambitious. By the early 1920s they owned three farms. Then, in 1925, the county drained a wetland and assessed owners of the land for the supposed improvement. Remarkably, the amount assessed was greater than the value of their farms, so the Rauenhorsts were forced into tenancy. When—in December of 1927 —their sixth son and seventh child, Gerald Anthony, was born, they were renting land north of Bird Island. A year later, the family moved again, to another tenant farm a mile west of Olivia. Three years after that, the family moved a third time, to a farm two miles farther west.

It was probably the memory of the last move that has lasted Gerry a lifetime: a small boy walking behind a wagon pulled by a team of horses, the wagon containing his family's earthly possessions, as the Rauenhorsts, deterred but not defeated, moved from one tenant farm to another.

And, while for some, such a recollection would be painful and embarrassing, for Gerry it is, well, "exciting." All these years later he explains: "Basically, I am an optimistic person. I don't look on the dark side of events. I look at almost everything—even if it's a disaster—as interesting. As *exciting*. As a challenge to work with and resolve."

As a small boy, he could not understand his parents' bad fortune, but he could appreciate the excitement of a move, of new sights and sounds, of a fresh adventure that began when the little procession stopped at the new farm and the family began unloading their wagon and began all over again.

Hard Times

But these were difficult times for the Henry Rauenhorst family, whether that's the way Gerry would remember it or not. As one of his older brothers, George, remarked in *The Things We Know Best*, an oral history of Olivia published in 1976:

"I remember once cleaning out the corn crib, shelling the ears of corn and running it in the coffee grinder. We ate corn mush for breakfast and fried mush for dinner and johnnycake for supper. That was field corn. We'd have that two or three days in a row, until the cream can got full enough to buy a sack of flour. We were getting by, so what the heck. People today, they'd be plum lost if they had to eat like that."

Still, it was not the Rauenhorsts' way to feel sorry for themselves. Endlessly resourceful and buoyed by their Catholic faith and their sheer, robust numbers, the family, George added, "just made up our minds that we weren't going to get beaten, that's all."

By 1929—as bad luck would have it, the beginning of the Great Depression—there were eight children on the premises. In the order of their births, they were William Cletus (known as Clete), Muriel, George, Jerome, Henry (called Hank), James (Jim), Gerald (Gerry), and Robert (Bob).

Muriel Rauenhorst Baumgartner recalls family life at the time:

> Our mother was a perfectionist. She kept everything going and wanted everything done just right. She kept everyone in line. Our dad worked awfully hard, but was a little easier-going than our mother.
>
> We didn't have a lot of money, but the farms were always productive. We always had plenty to eat. We butchered our own livestock. We had a big garden and had a basement full of the vegetables that we grew and canned. My mother was a good cook, as was her mother. I remember we ate very well.
>
> My mother had a difficult pregnancy with Gerry—I'm not sure why. Anyway, for that reason, Gerry was born at the University of Minnesota Hospital in Minneapolis. Because I was the only girl in the family, and because I was in high school by that time, it was my job to take care of the family while Mother was in Minneapolis. Then, when she and Gerry came home, Gerry and later Bob pretty much became my responsibility as Mother went back to the regular chores of a big farm family.

Margaret recovered her health and resumed her multifaceted role as nurturer, disciplinarian, and inspiration. She set the rules and ran the house, instilling in her children a rockribbed work ethic and integrity. "You never lied to my mom, or you lived to regret it," says Gerry. "For instance, when I got a bad report card, I would somehow lose it on the way home from school. Mom would ask, 'Where's your report card?' and I'd say, 'I don't know—I lost it.'

"Of course, she knew what I was doing, and the consequence was a spanking." While their father was no pushover, he was somewhat more lenient on the brood than his wife—or, at any rate, preoccupied with the day-to-day operations of the farm. She was in charge in and around the house, and a more constant presence in their children's lives, at least while they were small.

Meanwhile, Gerry and Bob, born barely thirteen months apart, were inseparable. They were so close, and so often dressed alike by their mother when they were young, that neighbors referred to them as the "Rauenhorst twins." Never mind that dark-haired Gerry was always smaller than his younger, redheaded brother.

The younger boys were, indeed, separated from the rest of their siblings by age: Jim, the next oldest, was seven years Gerry's senior. "It was almost a second family," Gerry recalls. "Our older brothers were always kidding around with us and throwing us in the air or something—always a lot of fun, even with the hard times and all the work we had to do."

From top to bottom, the Rauenhorsts were naturally entrepreneurial. Even in bad times, Gerry's father, Henry, was a shrewd risk-taker whose native optimism was encouraged by a good head for numbers, a sharp eye for a deal, and the energetic support of his wife and children.

In 1930, George agreed to take part in a potentially revolutionary research project developed by the University of Minnesota. As usual, the effort would be a family affair.

"The Rauenhorsts agreed to plant thirty acres of seed corn and to carry out the painstaking detasseling operation that would yield a hardier, more productive hybrid," write corporate historians Carol Pine and Susan Mundale. "In July, they manufactured a cart with parts from a cultivator and a rake, and hitched it up [behind] a horse. Jim drove the rig while Hank and George pulled tassels from four out of every six rows of corn.

"In the fall, when the hybrid corn was harvested, the brothers carried it in bushel baskets to the attic to dry. The following spring, the corn was shelled, graded, and bagged. Margaret's neat handwriting graced the labels. The bags were then sold to the Farmers' Seed and Nursery Company or to the few neighbors willing to try the new product. The Rauenhorsts' efforts would eventually become a full-fledged family enterprise—the Trojan Seed Company."

Gerry and Bob were only six and seven, respectively, when they began their first business together. Using a small pony-drawn buggy, they hauled freshly picked sweet corn from the family's field to a busy highway intersection not far from their home and sold $1.50 worth to passers-by. They had told neither their parents nor their siblings about the enterprise, yet when their elders found out they were, typically, pleased with the boys' gumption. And for a few years thereafter, the boys ran a small stand at the same location, earning money and teaching themselves how to run a business.

Said Gerry much later:

"We put our money in the bank, knowing it was for our education. Even though after two or three years we had no more than $100 in the bank, we were learning the value of money and saving."

He added: "In those days, money was short, but I never thought of us as poor."

The boys continued to learn while they earned. When they were ten and eleven, Bob and Gerry were enlisted to help out when brother George set up a small mink farm.

"It was our job to feed and take care of the mink," Gerry remembers. "We didn't know anything about the animals, so we read everything we could find. We learned that mink are carnivorous and that most people who raise them feed them rabbits. We found out that we could buy frozen jackrabbits by the gunnysack from South Dakota, where they were hunted and trapped for their pelts. It was an easy way to supply their food. But when those six mink each gave birth to six young, and we had almost forty mink to feed, we sometimes ran out of rabbits. More than once we found ourselves hunting at night for a jack-rabbit to feed the hungry mink."

But that was just part of this particular lesson. Gerry continues:

"That fall, we decided to go out of the mink business. We had the animals skinned and pelted, and when the pelts dried we decided the time had come to sell them. But George thought the price wasn't as good as it ought to be. He decided we would keep them through the winter, hoping for a better price in the spring. But when we were ready to sell in the spring, we found that bugs had gotten into the pelts and destroyed them. We salvaged just enough to break even.

"That taught me it's sometimes better to harvest what you have—to take a reasonable profit—than to hold out for more."

The earlier history picks up the story two years later, when the boys, again at George's initiation, began raising turkeys:

"The Rauenhorsts bought equipment—enough to house 2,400 turkeys at a time—from a turkey grower near Lamberton. Gerry was put in charge of the operation, and again his job involved research. He learned that after eight weeks the turkeys should be removed from the heated brooder houses and taken to an alfalfa field. He also learned they had to be moved every few days to fresh, clean grass to keep them free of disease. His research—and plenty of hard work—paid off in a successful first year's flock. Negotiating the deal himself, the young businessman sold the birds in the fall to Swift and Company.

"'We made enough to pay for the entire set-up, so the next year we raised two batches—4,000 turkeys—and planned to sell them to Swift that fall.'

"But market prices were low, so brother George decided to wait. And his decision would again be regretted. In November, a snowstorm struck suddenly, killing all but a thousand birds.

"Unlike the mink venture, however, the turkey operation was not abandoned. Gerry continued to increase the flock, learning the importance of maintaining accurate books and good relationships with bankers, as well as the need to pay attention to the turkeys.

"I owe a lot to my brothers—especially George—for insisting that I handle the entire operation," Gerry says. "It was excellent training. But there was a price. As a high school freshman, I really wanted to play football, so I tried out for the team. On about the second day of practice, George showed up at school and said, 'It's going to be turkeys, Gerry—not football.' So I went back to the turkeys."

("I wasn't too disappointed," Gerry quipped later, "because at 110 pounds, my future in football was not that bright.")

Yet the Rauenhorst boys were anything but singleminded.

In fact, their ability to spot opportunities quickly led them beyond agribusiness—and, after a fashion, provided Gerry with his first off-the-farm construction project while he and Bob were still in high school. Incredibly, the project was a 1,000-seat, concrete-block and wooden-plank "stadium" they built for Olivia's semi-pro baseball team; the team gave the boys, by way of compensation, rights to the stadium's concession stand for ten years. When the facility opened, the brothers bought an industrial corn popper in Minneapolis and shrewdly set it up under the bleachers, where the smell of fresh popcorn proved irresistible to fans. The boys also learned to salt the popcorn liberally, especially early in the game, thus ensuring a heavy demand for cold soda pop in the middle and late innings.

"The stadium cost us about $2,000 to build," Gerry recalled, "and in the first year we made almost enough to pay our expenses."

The brothers made enough in the stadium's second season to pay off the loan they'd needed to buy their building materials. And, when Gerry went off to college later that year, he sold his interest in the business to Bob.

"I got my investment out, and a little bit to boot," he says.

Lessons Learned

Though the Rauenhorst boys often operated as independent contractors, their various business ventures during the period were always part of the larger family effort to make it through the Great Depression. To that end, everybody did his or her part and, whatever the individual's interests, contributed to the collective good.

Margaret and Muriel, for instance, baked bread—as many as three dozen loaves a week—for the family and the occasional hired field hands. The women also tended the large garden, canned much of what they grew, and dutifully adapted the older siblings' hand-me-downs for the youngsters. Son Hank, to use another example, was a prodigious gardener in his own right, growing enough to require a few hired teens to help him and his younger brothers peddle the vegetables in town.

By the middle thirties, the family was planting almost a thousand acres of sweet corn under contract to a nearby canning company. The company said the boys could pick and sell the corn that matured before the factory was ready to process it.

But there was severe drought in 1936 and the corn was poorly pollinated, so the company ceased operations. Undaunted, the Rauenhorsts hitched a four-wheel trailer to their Model T and loaded it with imperfectly formed ears of corn. Still, they didn't have much luck peddling their harvest in the area. "We were chased out of one town for selling without a license," Jim remembered. "Sometimes we slept in a stubble field at night before getting rid of the corn the next day." Sometimes they bartered the corn for crates of peaches and raspberries, or for gasoline.

Hank finally suggested hauling the corn in the family's Chevrolet pickup to a farmers' market in the Twin Cities. There, they were so successful that Hank, who was eighteen, bought a new C-30 International truck, arranging with the local International Harvester dealer, Elmer Ferguson, to pay for the truck seventeen days later. The brothers then began a seventeen-day marathon. They would rise at four a.m., drive to the Jackson Street market in St. Paul, bag their corn (ten dozen ears to a bag), and sell the bags to grocers and housewives. They would often drive back to the farm at midday, fill the truck again, and return to St. Paul to sell more.

"We sold twenty-two loads in seventeen days before the market price fell from eighteen cents a dozen to something like nine cents," Jim recalled. "In a month, we had more than paid for that truck."

The family continued to grow and develop the hybrid corn started as part of the university research project. They struggled through the worst of the Depression, then began to make gains again as the economy gradually improved, selling the corn to dealers in St. Paul and Fargo, North Dakota. Eventually, the family built their own "seed house" where they dried and packaged what they had grown. Gerry and Bob, in addition to their other ventures, oversaw as many as 500 part-time "detasselers" hired from among their high school pals and other groups at thirty-five cents an hour.

The seed-corn enterprise continued to grow as the Depression gave way to the war economy of the early 1940s. The family's farming operation grew apace, so that by the early forties they were working some 2,000 acres of rented land. With the foresight that characterized their multiple efforts, they bought two new diesel tractors just days before the Japanese attacked Pearl Harbor, after which no such equipment would be easily available on the home front until the end of the war.

The war, of course, presented its own harsh demands, and when Hank, George, and Jim went into the service, their younger siblings had to take up the slack at home. Gerry, for instance, would come home from school at three in the afternoon, eat dinner, then work in the fields until two a.m., when he would be spelled by one of his brothers. He would sleep for a few hours, then get up for school, and begin the grueling schedule again.

Not that it was all work and no play, even during the most challenging times.

All the Rauenhorst kids went to school—Margaret and Henry made sure of that. For the first eight grades, they attended St. Aloysius Catholic school in Olivia. "There were four classrooms and four nuns," Gerry says. "My mom also made us take music lessons, so every other day we had to bring a box with three or four bottles of milk, eggs, and cheese for the sisters who gave us those lessons. I studied piano, but my ability as a musician was zero! I was just never any good at it. *None* of us was any good at it. But my mom wasn't trying to make us musicians. She just wanted us to know something about music. She wanted us to be well-rounded human beings, whether our future would be on the farm or some-where else. I also played the drums a little. And I carried a bass drum in the town parades. I wasn't very good at that either, but I had a pretty good time with it." After St. Aloysius, Gerry, like his siblings, attended Olivia's public high school.

There were several lakes nearby, so during the summer the family made frequent excursions to fish and swim in the cooling waters. The Rauenhorsts would also picnic with some of the family's dozens of relatives in the area. As Gerry recalls, "Often, on Sundays, we'd go with our mom and dad to their brothers' or sisters' farms—they were mostly *her* brothers and sisters—and we'd play with the kids, our cousins. Everybody had a big family in those days. We must have had about fifty cousins altogether."

At home, everybody came together around the dinner table—family members plus, more often than not, a half-dozen hired hands. And, despite the diversity of ages, interests, and talents, there was always the strong sense of familial love and connectedness that Henry and Margaret fostered through thick and thin. As busy as she was, Margaret, without fail, marked each of her children's birthdays during the year by baking one of her famous cakes. Margaret also found time to make sure the long, wearying hours in the field were rewarded with plenty of popcorn, candy, and other homemade treats.

Gerry was the runt of the family, three inches shorter than any of his brothers. But he rarely thought about his "disadvantage," or let it dissuade him from his work and other interests. In high school he played basketball on the B squad. On the farm he hauled around sacks of corn that were sometimes nearly as big as he was. His mother would get after the older boys when the chore—the lifting and carrying of 130-pound sacks of corn, for instance—seemed too much for Gerry, but Gerry shrugged off the help. That response seemed to be bred in the bone: The Rauenhorsts were big on cooperation, but didn't mind going it alone if they had to. And Gerry would get used to—would learn to thrive on—standing *figuratively* tall among the bigger boys and pulling his weight.

"I spent a lot of time driving a team of horses," he says. "Before we switched to tractors, which wasn't until I was a teenager, we did every-thing in the fields with horses and horse-drawn machinery. I did a lot, I remember, with a hay mower—a mower with a sickle, drawn by horses. I did a lot with a side-delivery rake, also horse-drawn. Of course, horses pulled the wagons. Eventually, we did have tractors, which I drove along with everybody else. In fact, while I was still pretty little, I got to be very handy on a tractor. One job I had for several summers was driving a trac-tor with a big hay fork on the front. I went down the windrows with the thing, picking up loads and dumping them to be piled by pitchfork on a haystack. I much preferred being on the tractor to being on the haystack.

"I was driving those horses by the time I was ten, the tractors as soon as we got them. It was fun, but it was serious business, too. The way I remember it, I was working all the time. *Everybody* was working all the time. And then, when the war started and three of my brothers went off to the service, the rest of us had to work all the harder. But no one complained. Everybody was willing to work. That's just the way it was in those days." The seasonal workload was large enough to include a pair of migrant workers from Mexico whom Gerry remembers as Moses and Amos. "They were nice people and hard workers," he says. "They came several years in a row."

Like his siblings—like most young people who grow up on a farm—Gerry was necessarily a jack-of-all-trades. But it was also apparent early on that he had both a passion and an aptitude for building things. He was naturally adept with a hammer and saw, and eagerly applied himself to construction projects ranging from turkey sheds to bleacher seats. In retrospect, he would realize that part of his motivation was simply making do when there wasn't the cash on hand to buy what was needed. But part of it was the sheer joy of working with his head and hands, of coming up with a practical plan and then, with the materials at hand, rendering that plan tangible.

So, as hard as life was for the Rauenhorst clan, the memories and lessons that Gerry carried with him from those early years would be overwhelmingly positive.

"We had just a wonderful life," he said decades later. "We were poor in material things—we didn't even have an indoor biffy until I was fifteen—but we were rich in the things that count.

"We were taught all the right things. To work hard and to not cheat and to always tell the truth. To treat people with respect, to pay your bills, and to go to church every Sunday.

"Those were lessons we learned—the habits we acquired—during those days on the farm."

College Days

Then, by the end of the summer of 1945, the war was over, and Henry and Margaret Rauenhorst's seven sons began setting out on their separate paths in the new post-war world. Their daughter, Muriel, had earned her nursing degree in 1938, married, moved to a farm near Bird Island, and begun a family of her own.

"It was our mother's fondest hope that her boys stay together," Gerry recalls, "but we were individualists, with entrepreneurial instincts, and we had to go our own way." At a family meeting when the older boys returned from the service, it was decided that George and Henry would run the burgeoning seed-corn operation while Clete, Jerome, and Jim would each receive one of the family's farms. Gerry and Bob were awarded $5,000 each for their contributions to the family business and would move on to college.

Actually, Gerry wanted to enlist when the war was still raging and most of the young men in his high school class, like his older brothers, were getting into uniform. But he was still only seventeen at the time, and his mother, determined that he continue his education, wouldn't sign the necessary papers for him. "You get down to St. Thomas and get in a semester first," she told him.

Gerry's collegiate preference—and, obviously, his mother's—was the College of St. Thomas in St. Paul (where Bob would join him two years later). There were several good reasons for that choice. St. Thomas was a small but respected, sixty-year-old Catholic institution, offering the kind of business and economics programs that interested Gerry, and it was close enough to home—a little more than an hour's drive—to minimize any concerns either party may have had about Gerry being too far removed from the farm. (Also, St. Thomas was then an all-male school, which may or may not have had anything to do with the decision.) So he enrolled in an accelerated three-year degree program and began classes in July 1945.

Gerry was already thinking about a career in engineering. "It was pretty simple," he explained later. "I was interested in building things." Because there wasn't an engineering program at St. Thomas, his business and economics studies there would serve as "pre-engineering" courses.

And, as it turned out, Gerry found the St. Thomas campus—located in a comfortable, middle-class section of the Minnesota capital a few blocks from the Mississippi River—a congenial spot to live and learn. Though he had been raised on the farm, he had spent enough time visiting the Twin Cities to fit in easily as an undergraduate.

As was the case at many colleges and universities in the 1940s, St. Thomas's dormitories housed military personnel during and shortly after the war—when Gerry arrived, only ninety of its 360 undergrads were civilians—and its classrooms were filled with newly returned servicemen making the most of a G.I. Bill education. Furthermore, because most Twin Cities students lived at home and commuted to campus, almost all of Gerry's civilian classmates who roomed on campus were out-of-towners like himself, from small-town and farm backgrounds much like his own. "It was a very comfortable setting," Gerry says. "Most of the people I got to know were the same as me—farmers' sons and guys from rural areas—so we had a lot in common right from the start."

Because of the crowding, Gerry moved into a large house owned by the college and known as The Annex, at the corner of Marshall and Prior, on the north edge of the campus. A friendly, goodhearted teacher named Joe O'Brien lived with his wife on the first floor, and, with the twenty-five to thirty young men who filled the three upper floors of the big frame structure, created a boisterous familial environment. The residents would come together for meals, study groups, and bull sessions. On some evenings, foursomes would gather to play bridge in the big living room. Occasionally, the bridge games would become marathons, at least one lasting for ten hours.

Gerry's contributions to the group included sacks of sweet corn that he'd bring back from weekend visits to the farm. "We'd put the corn in a big kettle in the kitchen and get out a pound of butter and sit there at the table and eat half a sack at a sitting," he says. "We had a lot of fun, but we worked hard, too. We were all basically good kids who were very involved in college."

One of Gerry's third-floor roommates was Leo Reding, a physical education major and an all-state halfback, and later a state legislator and mayor of Austin, Minnesota. More than fifty years later, Reding still remembers an incident that obviously impressed him—and says something, he believes, about the resourcefulness of his classmates.

"One night I came home, and Devere Traxler, Jack Marso, and Gerry were sitting around working on some physics problems for a class," he says. "The problems were really difficult, and nobody seemed able to solve them. Then, all of a sudden, Gerry got up and ran down to the drugstore on the corner and came back with a twenty-five-cent gyroscope—you know, one of those toys you get spinning with a string. Well, we played with the thing for about an hour and, believe it or not, we used it to help figure out those tricky problems. As I remember, most of that was Gerry's doing. He studied the damn thing and figured out the principle behind it and used it to solve the problems."

Gerry's inventiveness impressed Reding on more than one occasion during their college days. The first time Gerry took his pal home with him to the farm, Leo noticed a peculiar-looking contraption near an upstairs window in the Rauenhorst house. The device included a large fan and some kind of tank. When Reding asked about it, Gerry explained that on hot days he ran cold water through a garden hose up into the tank, then blew water-cooled air through the room with the fan in a rudimentary—but apparently effective—air-conditioning system.

Despite the money he'd received from his family on leaving home, Gerry worked odd jobs throughout his undergraduate years at St. Thomas. "Like many students, I had to work to get through college," he recalled later. "My first job was washing dishes at Ireland Hall, under the stern supervision of Camille Kirmser. But, because that didn't bring in much money, I also sold encyclopedias." After answering an ad in a St. Paul paper, he went to work for an outfit called the Collier Publishing Company, selling encyclopedias and other books door-to-door. He figured it was a good way to polish the salesmanship skills he'd first plied peddling sweet corn at home, "because," as he puts it today, "if you can sell encyclopedias, making cold calls on total strangers, you can probably sell anything."

Gerry and a half-dozen other young men were driven to a targeted neighborhood, where they would ring doorbells during two-hour shifts. "The key was getting into the house and telling the lady you were working your way through college," he explains. "Sometimes someone would buy an encyclopedia or one of the other books just to be nice." Gerry was a quick learner and apparently a persuasive pitchman, because the second week on the job he earned $65—no small amount in those days.

But after three months on the job, the strain of working a sales job and keeping up in the classroom was beginning to tell. Gerry suffered frequent colds, which he attributed to overexertion and a lack of sleep. Even his mother urged him to quit the job and concentrate on his studies. When he told his boss he was quitting, the man said, "You *can't* quit. You're the only real salesman I have. What are you going to college for, anyway? You're just wasting your time. You can sell anything." But Gerry had made up his mind, and thus ended his encyclopedia-selling career.

Gerry was, if for the first time in his life, a serious student. "I had gone through high school and, to tell the truth, hadn't opened a book until the day before I graduated," he admits. "But I had received reasonably decent grades because high school was very easy. At St. Thomas, which had much more rigorous standards, I learned you had to toe the mark. I could handle that, but I had to work at it. I had to study."

"The courses I took from Monsignor James Lavin and others in logic, theology, and religion would have an especially important influence in my life," he says. "The study of St. Thomas Aquinas's *Summa Theologica* and his five proofs of the existence of God gave my young mind a clearer understanding, and that is still very clear to me to this day."

Study he did (besides all the other things), and, eager to move on in life, he graduated, with a bachelor's degree in economics, in only three years. It was 1948. He was twenty years old.

"A Nice Girl, Just Your Type"

Gerry's life, however, could never be tracked linearly. Just as he was building an intellectual foundation for his career, he was also, in the spring of his second year at St. Thomas, beginning to develop a personal relationship that would be the keystone of his family life.

Gerry needed a date for the college's annual Tiger Homecoming, and one name that came to mind belonged to a young woman he had known of since they were kids. Her name was Henrietta Schmoll. Her parents, Henry and Sophia Schmoll, had farmed near Bird Island, not far from the Rauenhorsts. "I believe I first met her, years before St. Thomas, at the county fair in Bird Island," Gerry says. "My brother Bob was always telling me about this cute Schmoll girl. He kept saying, 'Gerry, you should get to know her. She's a nice girl, just your type.'

"Although our backgrounds were similar, her family had been a little better off than mine. They had a nice farm and a nice brick house, and, unlike us, they had indoor plumbing when she was born. Furthermore, they owned their farm, while we were tenant farmers. She was the youngest of the three Schmoll girls who were six years apart. But she worked hard on that farm, partly because her father wasn't always in good health and partly because that's the way she's been all of her life—energetic and a hard worker. She would go out and drive the tractor in the field all day, then come home, clean up, and go into town. She was such a cute little mite, but she was always strong and always got things done.

"Still," Gerry continues, "while I knew *of* her, I really didn't know her very well. My folks knew her folks more than she and I knew each other. What I knew was that the Schmolls were a really fine, decent family."

The lack of familiarity didn't keep Gerry from queuing up at a campus pay phone a couple of weeks before homecoming and calling Hanky's number. Hanky, by that time, had come to the big city, too. In fact, she was a home economics major at the College of St. Catherine, an excellent all-women's Catholic institution, a mile or so from St. Thomas.

Self-assured as he was, he was pleased and probably a little relieved when she accepted his invitation to the dance. Perhaps not surprisingly, she had been aware of him for many years, having seen him in town and heard her folks speak in a neighborly way about the Rauenhorsts. She later said she was neither surprised nor perturbed when he picked her up on homecoming night in the pickup truck he had borrowed from one of his brothers, which happened to be the only conveyance he could arrange for the weekend.

"He was very socially inclined, as were many of his friends at St. Thomas," Hanky would recall several decades later. "My roommate and I would double-date with Gerry and his friends. But it was Tiger Homecoming that put us together. And we just hit it off right from the beginning. Actually, we dated a lot after that. Sometimes we would just walk around campus—either St. Thomas or St. Kate's. Sometimes we'd walk over to Highland Park, which was a neighborhood nearby, and see a movie. Gerry didn't have his own car at that time, so if we didn't want to walk, he'd have to borrow someone's car or truck, or we'd take the streetcar. It was much simpler then, and a very happy time."

It was Gerry, by the way, who gave Hanky her distinctive nickname. When she was a freshman at St. Kate's, she waited tables for the campus food service. Upon learning her given name, her boss, Sister Adriana, for reasons apparently known only to herself, decided to call the young woman *Hank*. Later, on her first date with Gerry, all had been going well until she told him her nickname. Gerry said, "Gee, I might have a problem with that. My brother Henry is called *Hank*. I'm going to call you *Hanky*." Which he did—and which everybody else who knew and loved her did, too—from that day on.

And from that day on, Gerry never dated anyone else.

"Teaching...the One Thing I've Never Thought About"

For several years prior to their marriage, Gerry had been looking forward, with increasing concentration, to a career in engineering. He had applied to the engineering programs at both the University of Notre Dame in South Bend, Indiana, and the Massachusetts Institute of Technology in Boston. The former was filled with returning veterans, but MIT had an opening and accepted him. But now there were other factors to consider. Hanky had a year left before she would graduate from St. Catherine's, and, under the circumstances, Boston seemed a very long way from St. Paul.

After graduating from St. Thomas, in June 1948, a third, more convenient option was Marquette University in Milwaukee; the school not
only offered an excellent engineering curriculum, but was a relatively easy
drive from the Twin Cities. As it happened, Gerry's decision would be
facilitated by an unexpected arrangement suggested by a cousin, Vince
Keltgen, who lived near the Rauenhorst farm in Renville County. Keltgen
was a pilot. He owned a small airplane and needed help moving his hangar
to another site. He asked Gerry, who was back home temporarily working
on his family's farm following graduation, to help. In exchange, Vince said,
he would teach the younger man how to fly. Gerry agreed to the deal.
He and Leo Reding helped Keltgen disassemble and transport the hangar
to its new location, and Keltgen taught Gerry how to fly.

Within two months, Gerry, ever the quick study, had acquired his
pilot's license. And then he bought Keltgen's plane—a sixty-five horse-
power, war-surplus 058B Grasshopper made by Aronca—for $500. Similar
to the familiar Piper Cub, the little plane had neither a battery nor a
generator, nor any modern instruments because it had no electricity. "To
start it, you cranked it by hand," Gerry recalls. "You used a stick to control
it, and kept track of your fuel by looking out the window at the gas gauge—
which was a cork in a tube. As rudimentary as it was, though, I never ran
out of gas, never experienced a dangerous situation, never had to make an
emergency landing. Actually, the greatest danger was getting hit by the
propeller when you cranked it!"

At the time, Gerry barely had enough money to go back to school,
but his cousin Vince, whose need for cash was apparently even greater than
Gerry's, made it an offer he couldn't refuse. Gerry, moreover, recognized
that Milwaukee would now be only a short hop from St. Paul. So everything was falling into place. Gerry was admitted to Marquette's engineering
program and worked in the family's seed-corn business until there was a
vacancy, then began attending class in Milwaukee in December 1948.

If St. Thomas had been a significant leap from high school in Olivia,
Marquette's engineering courses were Gerry's stiffest academic challenge
to date. Not only were the courses intrinsically difficult, but the large

numbers of older, more experienced, and just as ambitious men seeking a rewarding civilian career after several years of military service provided tough competition for grades. Gerry worked hard, but found himself on academic probation before the halfway mark of his first year. "I was sorely disappointed," he says. "I felt I was a failure. I thought about dropping out and getting a job, perhaps in the seed business with my brothers."

At the end of his first semester, he hitched a ride home with his brother Clete, who was en route to Olivia from a business trip in Chicago. Angry and frustrated, Gerry vented his feelings. "I did most of the talking all the way home," he recalls. "Clete was mostly silent. Every once in a while he'd say, 'Oh, is that so?' Or, 'Uh-huh, uh-huh.' But by the time we got home he'd let me talk myself out of quitting." Gerry smiles and adds: "Clete was a very special guy and a pretty good amateur psychologist. He was about nineteen years older than I was and never had children of his own, so I was kind of his special guy. We were very close, and I trusted his judgment."

So, with Clete's quiet encouragement, Gerry refocused on an academic future. "I thought, 'Gee, I'm twenty years old. I won't be a happy man when I'm fifty if I don't pursue an engineering career.' So I just decided to go back and get my engineering degree because that's what I'd started out to do and because that's what I liked." And that's what he did. Back at Marquette, he brought up his grade-point average, got off probation, and more than held his own with his brainy, ambitious classmates.

He would have no second thoughts, ever, about the branch of engineering he chose. "I never wanted to go into electrical engineering, for instance," he says. "I always wanted to be a building—a civil—engineer. Remember, I always liked building things, because, when you're finished, you have something tangible, something you can look at and walk around and touch. It's a creative endeavor, but when it's done, people can use it, so it's practical as well. I've always believed that people should try to do what they like to do, and this is what I thought I'd like to do."

Gerry found a novel way to help pay for school while broadening his social relationships: He taught several of his Marquette classmates how to fly, charging $5 for a one-hour lesson in his little plane. It wasn't long, for that matter, before he had recouped the Grasshopper's purchase price and considered it one of the best investments of his fledgling business career.

The airplane proved, in the meantime, to be as valuable to his relationship with Hanky as he had hoped. He flew home often, landing at Holman Field near downtown St. Paul. He'd pick up Hanky, who had graduated from St. Catherine's and taken a good job as a home economist at Northern States Power Company in Minneapolis, and proceeded home to Bird Island and then Olivia. Eventually, the couple began talking seriously about getting married.

Then, once again, an unexpected problem and unlikely opportunity presented themselves, one connected to the other.

Gerry and Hanky had made marriage plans. He would find a job after graduating in August, and they would get married in September. But when registering for his spring quarter classes, Gerry learned that two courses he needed to complete his degree were scheduled at the same time. He would have to go back to Marquette in the fall to take one of them.

"I can't wait around to take that one course," he told O. Neal Olson, who headed the school's engineering department. "I'm getting married in the fall. By then, I want to be out of here and in a job."

"Have you ever thought about teaching?" Olson asked. One of his youngest and most resourceful students, Gerry had the makings of a good engineer and Olson was personally fond of him.

Gerry looked at the older man blankly. "Teaching?" he echoed. "That's the one thing I've *never* thought about."

Olson explained that he was short a civil engineering instructor, that he felt Gerry, despite his inexperience, was good enough to teach the subject, and that Gerry could teach and take his remaining classes at the same time. Gerry would get a salary, of course, but also free tuition, so he could get married and then graduate at the end of winter quarter.

Within a few weeks, Gerry, at the ripe old age of twenty-two, was a full-time instructor in Marquette's School of Engineering. Never mind that the average age of his students was twenty-five. Dean Olson, for his part, was pleased, and added two new classes to Gerry's teaching load in each of the next two quarters. By the time he graduated, in March 1951, Gerry was teaching five courses a quarter and still earning $260 a month. He would later say he learned more about engineering by teaching it than he did as a student.

One of the courses he taught near the end of his Marquette career was called Civil Engineering Problems; the course was designed to prepare students for the engineering registration exam required by the state of Wisconsin. Dean Olson asked Gerry to teach the course he normally taught because the University of Wisconsin students were scoring higher than the Marquette students, and Olson thought a change of instructors might result in an improvement in scores. Gerry taught the course in the spring and summer of 1950, and, when he took the two-part state exam along with his students, he scored a perfect one hundred on the first section and ninety-two on the second. What's more, his Marquette students, as a group, outscored their counterparts at the University of Wisconsin, where the test had been developed! Needless to say, Olson was pleased.

Not that Gerry's graduate education was all a grind. For one thing, O. Neal Olson himself had a wry sense of humor. Gerry remembers the time, during a party at which a substantial amount of alcohol had been consumed, when a slightly defiant student named Jack Love issued the dean a challenge. "Olson," Jack said, "I can do anything you can do, and I can do it better!" To which Olson replied, "Can you really?" When Jack assured him he could, Olson stepped back from the bar, pulled out a jack knife, and stabbed himself in the leg. The dean, it turned out, had a wooden leg.

Gerry got into the spirit of things at his class's graduation party, which Olson and a number of Gerry's friends attended, at Triangle, the engineering fraternity. "I wasn't much of a drinker," Gerry says, "but I was a prof and I was graduating, so I had to be part of the festivities. Before I went to the party I ate everything fatty I could find. I asked Hanky to fix me a slice of bread with a half-inch of butter on top, and ate that down, too.

"Well, at the party we consumed a lot of martinis, though I managed to slop at least some of mine out of the glass while I was drinking. Somehow I managed to survive the evening. But the next morning I climbed out of bed and promptly fell over. Seems the booze was just then making its way through all the butter!"

The Journey of a Lifetime

In the meantime, there had been one more hitch in Gerry and Hanky's carefully constructed plans for a September 1950 wedding. This time the hitch was created by the draft board.

First, a tad more family history. Gerry's mother, remember, wouldn't sign for him when he had wanted to enlist during the war. When, in December 1945, he turned eighteen, however, he was eligible for the draft and ordered to report to Fort Snelling for a physical and, presumably, induction.

"I was a freshman at St. Thomas by that time, but I was ready to go," Gerry recalls. "I said goodbye to my folks, packed a duffel bag, and reported to the barracks with my college friend Don McGuire. When we were given our physicals, Don was ahead of me in line. He was handed a white card, and I got a red card. I said, 'Hey, give me a white one, too. I want to go the same place he's going.' But the guy in charge said, 'You're not going anywhere except home. You're 4-F.'" A doctor told Gerry he had a pilonidal cyst—a congenital growth at the base of his spine. His own doctor at the time confirmed the diagnosis, but told him not to worry about it. The cyst was benign.

But about a year later the cyst began to hurt, and Gerry eventually had to have it removed. The procedure left him recuperating in the hospital, lying flat on his stomach for two weeks, then required another five months to heal completely. And once recovered, he was no longer 4-F.

Almost four years passed. When the Korean War broke out in the summer of 1950, Gerry had been reclassified 1-A, which meant that in the Army's eyes he was physically able for military duty. "In August, I got my notice from the draft board," he says. "'Report to Fort Snelling on September 1,' it said. Well, I went down there, stayed all day, then came back home in the evening—just in time for our wedding rehearsal. The rule was you didn't have to go in if you were married, and I was able to convince the draft board that we had been planning our wedding long before I received my notice. While I had been very eager to go in the first time, I wasn't so eager to go in now."

So as per their plan, albeit with a few corrections and adjustments, Hanky and Gerry were married on September 2, 1950, at St. Mary's Catholic Church in Bird Island. It was a bright sunny day in Renville County, and both families, plus numerous friends, looked on approvingly. His brother Bob was Gerry's best man, and Hanky's best friend, Rita Gillach, was the maid of honor.

For their honeymoon, the newlyweds drove to the Canadian Rockies and Lake Louise. It was the first of many trips they would take together —and the start of a journey that would last a lifetime.

Chapter Two

Building

When Gerry emerged from academe to start his engineering career (as much as he enjoyed, and had learned from, his teaching experience at Marquette, he never seriously considered making education his career), America was hard at work in a booming economy after the war. Not surprisingly, given his entrepreneurial genes, Gerry dreamed of running his own business someday, but he understood that he first needed some real-world experience working for someone else.

Fortunately, in 1951, a bright young civil engineer did not have to look too hard or too long to find a job. Many of the possibilities were government positions, but Gerry wasn't interested in sitting behind a desk as part of a sprawling bureaucracy. He wanted a job where he was, in his words, "actually doing something...being productive." Then one day, during his final quarter at Marquette, a classmate walked up to him and said his father-in-law, a contractor, was looking to hire an engineer. Could Gerry recommend one of his students for the job?

Gerry had just the candidate in mind. He thought, "Wow, this is my big opportunity. Here I go!"

"The Optimism of Youth..."
Thus Gerry began his first professional job in August 1951, handling the bidding for a contractor in a small Wisconsin city. The job paid $80 a

week and gave him the opportunity to learn about the construction business in general and the bidding process in particular.

He and Hanky—who gave up the home economist's job with the Wisconsin Gas Company she had landed after moving from the Twin Cities to Milwaukee—took up residence in a small apartment in a converted candy factory not far from where he worked. The future seemed bright. After years of school and struggle, they were finally on their own, financially independent of their families. And, in December 1951, the future came to life in the person of a baby girl, who was born in the hospital across the street from their apartment and christened Judith Mary Rauenhorst. Gerry would look back on that cold winter day as one of the happiest of his life.

But, almost immediately, he was troubled by his employer's operations. The man's approach to both business and his personal life was, in fact, offensive to Gerry, whose family background and academic experience had placed honesty, ethical practices, and personal morality ahead of all other considerations. No job, Gerry decided and Hanky concurred, was worth compromising the principles that guided his life. So Gerry quit the job, and he, Hanky, and baby Judy headed back to Minnesota.

After reviewing local phone books for the names of construction companies, then sending out fifty letters (carefully typed, stamped, and posted by Hanky), Gerry was offered, and accepted, an estimator's job at a salary of $100 a week. But, again, he was quickly disenchanted by the conduct of his employer. Returning home from work troubled by philosophies and business practices he couldn't change and angry with what he was seeing and hearing during the day, he poured out his thoughts over dinner with Hanky and said, more than once, "There just has to be a better way."

From a business point of view, "a better way" would mean, he decided, making an honest, realistic bid for a project and then sticking to that bid no matter what. It would mean showing up when he said he was going to show up, and finishing a job when promised. Personally, it would mean treating clients, co-workers, and employees with honor, decency, and respect, keeping your word, and behaving according to the highest moral standards.

After only a couple of months on the job, Gerry began weighing his options and thinking through alternative courses of action. It was not his way to make rash decisions or to act without a carefully considered plan. Eventually, he and Tom Stevenson, another unhappy young man at the firm, decided to start a construction company on their own time. Calling themselves Trojan Construction (an obvious echo of the Rauenhorst family's Trojan Seed Company), they began bidding on projects in the fall of 1952. Both of their first two bids were rejected.

Then, in January, Gerry learned that the congregation of Zion Lutheran Church in, of all places, Olivia was interested in building a new house of worship. Where better than his hometown to break ground for the first time and construct his first building, Gerry mused. But, while the two men were researching the Zion project, Stevenson became seriously ill and decided to drop out of their partnership. "But I think you should go ahead," he told Gerry. "I know you can do it." Accustomed to operating on his own when he had to, Gerry went ahead.

First, however, he turned to a trusted advisor: his brother Clete. "The bid will be a little over $55,000," he told him. "I'll need a certified check for $2,850 for a bid bond. [The law required contractors to put up five percent of the bid to guarantee their proposal.] I have $354. Could you lend me $2,500?"

When Gerry returned to Minneapolis that night, he had Clete's check in his pocket. He prepared the bid and, because he was still working for somebody else, asked Clete to deliver it.

The chilly winter afternoon the bids were opened, the old Olivia church hall was filled with anticipation. One by one the figures were examined. Finally, the building chairman announced that the low bid had been submitted by Trojan Construction Company.

"Who is Trojan Construction Company?" the church fathers asked, almost as a chorus.

"Trojan Construction is my brother Gerry," Clete Rauenhorst replied from the back of the room.

That night on the phone Clete told Gerry, "You're $5,000 under the next guy. But he's a good Lutheran, so there may be some trouble."

A month later, Gerry appeared before the church fathers—men he had known since his childhood. Clete, moreover, had gone to school with the building chairman, which didn't hurt Gerry's chances. But the chairman's brother wanted the church to be built by a Lutheran; he also said he had reservations about Gerry's youth and inexperience.

When it was his time to speak, Gerry acknowledged the committee's doubts. "I know I'm asking you to let a twenty-five-year-old build the church you've saved a lifetime for," he said. "All I can say is that you have my certified check, and if you decide to give me the contract, you will have a performance bond that will guarantee I'll build the church for the amount stated. If I don't, you're entitled to keep my $2,850. You'll have to decide."

Afterwards, Gerry waited outside until the group made its decision. "The job is yours," the chairman said at last. "By a vote of twenty-four to sixteen."

"The Rauenhorst family's credibility and Gerry's earnest determination had convinced the committee that he was right for the job," Pine and Mundale wrote later. "But not every committee member was a believer. The chairman asked for [a second] vote to demonstrate unanimity. That vote was twenty-three to seventeen. Wisely, he decided to stop asking for votes and start planning to build. Despite a last-minute offer by the building chairman's brother to pay the $5,000 difference and give the job to the next lowest bidder, Gerry's construction company landed its first contract."

The Zion Lutheran job in hand, Gerry resigned his estimator's position with the firm that had been employing him and declared himself independent. Not everyone thought that was a sound decision. He was, after all, only twenty-five years old—and looked even younger. He had an engineering degree from a prestigious university, but precious little on-the-job experience in a rough-and-ready, highly competitive, high-stakes industry. He also had a wife and two small children (the couple's first son, Mark, was born in February 1953) and would be operating without the safety net of a family fortune.

But there were encouraging voices, too. One older man by the name of Art Solly, at the Stewart Lumber Company in Minneapolis, told him, "When I was your age, I thought about going out on my own, but people said, 'Why don't you wait a year or so until things get better?' Well, I waited and waited, and you know what? Things never got better. The dumbest thing I ever did was not start that business. So I say go for it."

"I knew I was taking a risk, but I guess I had the so-called optimism of youth," Gerry recalled decades later. "A part of me thought, 'If this doesn't work, I'll be digging ditches for a long time'—but I really didn't have a great fear of failing. I think I was more worried about getting an individual job done than I was about failing at the business. I knew I didn't have much experience, but I also knew I'd get experience by doing things. I just thought, 'Well, if I work hard enough and do things right, it's going to come out all right.'"

From the start, Gerry enjoyed the wise and seasoned counsel of his older brothers. George and Hank, who were building the Trojan Seed operation into a major business, gave sage advice. Hank would also kid Gerry about the comparative ease of starting a construction firm. In the seed business, Hank teased, you had to have all these fields and plants and capital, while in construction "all you needed was a truck and a wheelbarrow." Brother Clete, meanwhile, remained a man of few words—but invariably helpful ones. Clete continued to be, in fact, an invaluable mentor to his young, ambitious, but untested brother, hearing him out and quietly advising him on a range of important matters.

For the Zion church project, Gerry subcontracted a construction crew, plasterers, and painters, and began seeking out material suppliers, with a sharp eye, despite his inexperience, for quality and value. That Lutheran church, he promised himself, would be the best building he could possibly build. And, as the church's congregation would eventually agree, it was an excellent building indeed.

Winning Bids, Growing the Business

By the end of April 1953, Gerry was in business for himself.

He was supporting a wife and two young ones, and working out of the little family's first house—a 960-square-foot, three-bedroom bungalow at 6427 18th Avenue South in Richfield, a modest suburb just south of the Minneapolis line. The house had cost Gerry and Hanky about $11,000. They paid back a loan for the house's down payment by working extra jobs—Hanky, a talented seamstress, doing alterations and reweaving damaged garments for a local dry cleaning shop and Gerry selling life insurance.

In his "spare time," Gerry built a two-car garage on the property and connected it to the house with an eight-by-sixteen-foot breezeway that he would use for his office—the first headquarters of the fledgling business.

Much of his workday, early on, was spent preparing bids for construction jobs. "The day before a bid was due I'd take out the plans and refamiliarize myself with them," he explains. "I would check to make sure all the sub-bids were in—generally twenty to thirty bids from other people. Then, after a day's work, I would come home, have dinner, and go to sleep, often on the living room floor. When Henrietta went to bed at eleven or twelve, she would wake me. I would get up, go to my office, and often work all night. It was quiet then—no phones ringing, no kids, no visitors. By eight the next morning, I would have all my quantities organized—tons of bricks, yards of concrete, feet of lumber. As soon as I could, I'd begin calling to double-check my sub-bids. Then I would add everything up and take it all to the bid opening. There could be as many as twenty-five bidders for each job, so to get jobs you had to bid often."

The lowest bid did not always result in the job. Gerry quickly learned that other, less tangible factors would be important in getting a bid and building his business.

There was, for example, St. Raphael's Catholic parish in suburban Crystal that, in 1954, wanted to build a convent for its teaching sisters. Gerry's bid was the lowest, but the church's architect believed the job should go to another builder.

"What do you know about this kid?" the architect asked Father Frank Fenelon, the parish priest.

"Not much," the priest replied, "but I think I'd like to talk to him."

In Fenelon's office, with the architect present, Gerry stated his case.

When he finished, Fenelon said, "I'm going to give it to the kid because I like him." It would be the beginning of a long and productive relationship. It would also be typical of the way Gerry would conduct business through-out his career—plainspoken, persistent, and difficult to turn down once he'd laid out his proposal.

Gerry bid frequently, though not always successfully, on projects planned by the St. Paul-Minneapolis archdiocese. In fact, during one stretch early in his career, Gerry lost out on five consecutive Catholic school projects (each time to a builder who eventually went out of business—the victim, evidently, of persistent lowballing). But one memo-rable victory involved the bid for a convent attached to the Catholic church in Albany, Minnesota. Gerry had bid against several nearby companies, but when he arrived home after a meeting late one night, he found a note pinned to his pillow.

"Wake me up," Hanky had written.

When he woke her, she exclaimed, "We got the job!"

The couple celebrated their unexpected triumph with a toast, using a bottle of blackberry brandy they'd found in a kitchen cupboard. A blackberry brandy toast thus became the traditional celebration in the Rauenhorst firm and family.

That Albany job, as it happened, marked the beginning of a real company, with employees, as compared with a one-man operation. Strictly speaking, of course, the company had never been a one-person operation, inasmuch as Hanky had been answering the company phone, receiving supplies, handling the firm's correspondence and invoicing, and writing checks for subcontractors. In that sense, the firm was a *family* business from the get-go. But, in 1954, it became a "real" company with a boss and employees, with the hiring, first, of a highly respected construction superintendent named Elmer Sandeen to oversee the Albany convent project and then Sandeen's son Tom, followed by Sandeen's son-in-law, Gerry Grimm, and another man, Dick Billmeier, who would work for the company for almost fifty years.

The hirings reflected Gerry's desire to grow his operation, which was soon rechristened Rauenhorst Construction. (The name change was intended to both underscore the owner's personal accountability and avoid any possible confusion with the family's seed-corn enterprise.) Work was plentiful in Minnesota during the middle fifties. In fact, the company's volume doubled each year for the next several years, and Gerry continued adding field employees to keep pace. The paperwork required by the additional work necessitated still more staff—there was far more office work than Hanky, with her growing family, could or wished to handle— and Gerry hired the firm's first full-time office manager, an experienced bookkeeper named Marcel Sciez.

In 1955, Gerry built the company's first dedicated headquarters, at 7848 Fremont Avenue South in south suburban Bloomington. The 5,000-square-foot, single-story building replaced the breezeway office at their Richfield home, which, by that time, was bursting at the seams with four children under the age of six. (As one observer noted, "Suppliers and contractors calling the business at the Richfield house were likely to hear the sound of the washing machine running in the background.") Half of the new building was leased to another company, marking the beginning of leasing as a part of the business. The project also marked the first time the company bought land.

That land transaction taught Gerry another valuable lesson. There were two parcels for sale at the site, for $2,500 each. Gerry bought one and designed the building twice as large as the company needed, planning to rent out the other half. As it happened, three companies were interested in the space, so Gerry signed up one of them and made plans to erect a second building on the adjacent site for the other two. But when he proffered a check for $2,500, the landowner said in effect, "Sorry, but the improvements you made have doubled the value of the land. The second parcel will now cost you *$5,000.*" Then and there, Gerry promised himself that he would secure as much land as he might possibly need *before* building.

Despite the miscalculation, Rauenhorst Construction had turned a corner and become a significant player in the local construction industry, with its own building and a growing staff and field operation. By 1957, the company was bidding on and building a range of buildings, from churches and schools to small office buildings and warehouses—even a couple of private homes. By the *end* of 1957, in fact, the firm had completed more than fifty buildings around the state, for such diverse clients as the Trojan Seed Company, the University of Minnesota, the Mutual Creamery Insurance Company, Pure Oil, the National Farm Loan Association, the Knights of Columbus, Interstate G.M. Diesel, Luger Boats, and numerous churches, schools, and convents of the local archdiocese.

They weren't enormous or ostentatious structures, any of them, but they all bore the solid craftsmanship and meticulous attention to detail for which the company was already well-known.

John McKeown, one of Gerry's Marquette University classmates, fraternity brothers, and flight students, came aboard as engineer and estimator. And, on November 14, 1957, the firm formally incorporated, with Gerry as president and treasurer, McKeown as vice president, Sciez as secretary, and Hanky as assistant secretary. (Gerry later liked to call her his first chief financial officer, but that was a title she never, in fact, formally held.) A local attorney named George Connor handled the incorporation process, and, like the others, would enjoy a long association with Gerry and the firm.

A year later, another long and important association began—or, more accurately put, was *renewed*—when Gerry bid on and secured the contract to build Dowling Hall, a dormitory that would house 340 students at the College of St. Thomas in St. Paul. And, while that project was under way, the company bid on the college's new student union, Murray Hall.

As usual [according to a company report] Gerry stayed up all night calculating his bid. The next afternoon more than 150 people—mostly contractors and subcontractors—filled the college's auditorium for the opening of the bids. Gerry put his bid on the desk, then sat down next to Charlie McGough, one of his competitors. The first ten bids were opened; Gerry knew his was still the lowest. "But I had to wait until nearly the end of the process before McGough's bid was read, and then I was relieved because I considered him our strongest competition." When all the bids were open, Gerry stepped to the front of the room, shook hands all around, and went home to dinner.

He had been awake for twenty-three hours straight, but he wanted to watch the ten o'clock news before he turned in. He stretched out on the living room floor in front of the television. A short time later, the doorbell rang. Standing on the front step were St. Thomas president, Dr. James Shannon, and the college's dean, Monsignor William O'Donnell. They told Hanky that they had been caught up in the drama of the afternoon's events— the auditorium filled with observers, the suspense as the envelopes were opened, the bids themselves, each one so carefully calculated. Now, the callers said, they wanted to see what the winner was doing to celebrate.

The winner was sound asleep on the living room floor, but he awoke long enough to offer a toast of blackberry brandy to his unexpected guests.

The Design/Build Concept

Gerry continued to develop his business—erecting larger and more complex structures for local churches, schools, and corporations— during the late 1950s and into the sixties. Thinking outside the normal construction executive's mindset, he was picturing himself expanding the operation in several directions at once.

But it was the decision to become a turnkey—better described as *design/build*—operation that changed everything for the still relatively small builder, and provided both the operating concept and functional apparatus for the remarkable growth that followed.

Gerry had long been impatient, and often frustrated, with the traditional bidding process. He believed that design/build offered a clearly superior alternative. He would later describe and contrast the processes like this:

In the traditional or sequential method of contracting, a construction company comes into a building project after someone else has already drawn the architectural plans and completed the engineering design. The builder's job is limited to constructing from those plans. In some instances, the construction company is asked to both design and construct the facility. In such a case, the contractor engages independent architects and engineers to design the building, and then builds from those plans.

In the case of a design/build firm, full responsibility for design and construction is assumed by the company, utilizing either an in-house or, in some cases, an outside staff of architects and engineers or retaining outside specialists. By serving as the single source of responsibility for a construction project, the design/build firm is able to be involved in and manage the design, and closely coordinate personnel and materials, thus accelerating and scheduling with precision the ultimate completion date and maintaining budget control. In addition to effecting savings on interim construction financing, this enables the owner to maintain on-line operations with minimum delay and disruption, getting the client out of the old building and into the new facility at a predetermined time.

Practicing what he preached, Gerry would eventually grow his operation into what he described as "a totally integrated firm employing architects, engineers, construction specialists, and specialists in finance, real estate, and building management." He could soon tell prospective clients: "We have the in-house design talent, engineering expertise, and, in the field, construction professionals to take your project from the conceptual state to completion." While each job is different, "design/build is committed to create the best solution."

Gerry began to consistently apply the design/build concept to major projects in 1961, when Rauenhorst built the Toro Company's office and warehouse facility in Bloomington. And, as would often be the case as

Gerry's company developed, one opportunity quickly led to others, and Gerry had the opportunity to show the imagination and resourcefulness that would stand him in good stead for the big years ahead.

Actually, Gerry had experimented with the concept in 1958, when Rosemount Engineering asked him to build a new facility. He first found suitable land for the project in the vicinity of Highways 100 and 5, in the still mostly rural southwestern corner of the Twin Cities. "We bought seventeen acres owned by Bradley Trust of Boston," Gerry recalls. "Bradley was the first REIT [real estate investment trust] formed in the United States, and at the time a REIT couldn't own raw land, so they had to sell." Rauenhorst Construction designed and built Rosemount Engineering's new plant on the site, plus another building and a new headquarters for itself (at 5000 West 78th Street). But Bradley Trust still had 200 acres of undeveloped land in the area that it was eager to sell.

"Darrell Holt, who was the head of Towle Realty, kept calling, saying I really should buy it," Gerry says. "But I didn't want to take a risk on that much raw land. Finally, I took stock of the situation and thought, 'Well, what can I risk? The answer was, $20,000. I could afford to lose that.' So I offered to give them the $400,000 they were asking, with five percent—that's $20,000—down and five percent interest, but no interest or principle payments for five years. It may not have been the best deal for them, but it was the only offer they were getting, and they accepted.

"So we bought that land for $20,000 down," he continues. "It was an interesting situation. Part of the land was in Edina, and part of it was in Bloomington. Bloomington was closer to the river and lay lower than Edina. So I asked Edina if it would supply all the water for the new projects, because water runs downhill. I asked Bloomington if it would handle the sewage. And, though I had never heard of an arrangement quite like that, both communities agreed."

Also, at that time, the land in Edina was zoned residential, while the land in Bloomington was industrial, which meant that on the municipal line you could be building factories across the street from fine houses. "I told Edina I'd build a golf course adjacent to their residential piece if they would rezone the piece on the other side to industrial," Gerry says. "That way I'd have some industrial-zoned sites on my Edina land and there would be a golf course buffer between the industrial and the houses. They accepted that, too."

By today's standards, the development of the area was incredibly swift. "We completed the land deal in March and began laying out the water, sewer, and streets by May," as Gerry tells it. "Then Control Data came along, and we made a deal with Tom Kamp, president of their Magnetic Controls division, to build a new factory on the site, and we had that finished in September. It was amazing, really. Today that process would take at least five years, but we just went ahead back then and did it. Obviously, the economies of moving that fast were enormous. And it was done right—as good as it could be done today. It's just that we were geared up to do it [as a design/build operation] and there wasn't all the governmental bureaucracy and red tape there is today."

Rauenhorst built and leased other parcels on the site, which became the company's first large industrial development: Normandale Industrial Park. "The parcels sold rapidly, we built other buildings, and within about a year and half we had paid off the entire $400,000 [purchase price]," Gerry explains. "We were going to build what is now the Radisson South Hotel on the site, but the parcel we were going to build it on was in Bloomington, which wouldn't allow liquor sales at the time," he adds. "So instead, we built the first Howard Johnson's [motor hotel and restaurant] west of the Mississippi River, which did not serve liquor. The following year, Bloomington voted to allow the serving of spirits, so I went to Howard Johnson headquarters in New York and asked if I could put in one of their restaurants that served liquor. They refused, so on an adjacent site we built the Camelot restaurant, which was, for a while, one of the top fifty restaurants in the country and served our Howard Johnson's customers who wanted a fine dinner and a drink."

(When Gerry went back to New York to secure a franchise for a second Twin Cities HoJo's, this one in St. Paul, Howard Johnson Jr. was decidedly unfriendly. "You built a restaurant that serves liquor next to our Bloomington hotel, and we don't like that," Johnson said. "I'll bet you're broke in two years." When Gerry shot back, "How much do you want to bet?" Johnson said nothing. As it turned out, Rauenhorst was awarded the second HoJo franchise in St. Paul—and the Camelot was a thriving concern for many years to come.)

Like most successful entrepreneurs, Gerry had the gift of long vision—but he would be the first to admit that he was *not* following a grand plan. If there was a plan at all, he was making it up as he went along, his eyes peeled for future developments and ever ready to take advantage of unanticipated opportunities as they presented themselves.

They didn't have to be huge opportunities like Normandale Industrial Park, either, he says, smiling at the memory of another, somewhat more modest transaction during the early 1960s.

Gerry was preparing to develop more than a hundred acres of highly valuable land he had purchased along France Avenue in Edina and in the meantime was selling gravel off the site.

"Well, it turned out that the guy who was buying the gravel couldn't pay his bill, so he gave me his black Lincoln as payment," Gerry says. "It was the fanciest car I had owned to date. We took the kids on trips in it."

A Lean Team and Savvy Mentors

As fast as his business was growing during its first several years, Gerry insisted on running a lean operation. Even while his field operations were rapidly expanding, he maintained a full-time office staff of only McKeown, Sciez, and receptionist-secretary Martha Durocher.

The next major addition was a twenty-two-year-old engineer recently graduated from Marquette named Nick Simons, who, decades later, would laugh and shake his head when recalling his first meeting with Rauenhorst Construction's management on the university's campus in Milwaukee. Instead of sitting stiffly for a formal interview, Gerry and John McKeown, in their shirt sleeves, were busy studying a set of blueprints when Simons walked in.

Later, when visiting company headquarters in Bloomington, Simons was offered a Braunschweiger sandwich for lunch and put to work double-checking figures for a bid that was due that afternoon. The unlikely combination of friendly informality and task-oriented professionalism impressed the young engineer, who, until meeting Rauenhorst, had not been interested in either a job in the construction business or moving to the Twin Cities. Once on the payroll, he would say later, "I did everything from calculating structural components to doing architectural drafting to buying out subcomponents of jobs and managing construction."

Simons' arrival in 1960 marked an early watershed—and diversification—for the company. "Its major projects at the time included the dormitory at the College of St. Thomas, the library at the College of St. Catherine, Annunciation Church in Minneapolis, and a seminary building at Nazareth Hall Day School in St. Paul," an early company history noted. "When [Simons] returned following six months of Marine Corps training in the late spring of 1961, Rauenhorst had moved completely away from bidding on jobs to doing both design and construction."

Simons would then be involved in both the design and construction of the new Toro Company manufacturing plant in Bloomington and a processing facility for the Gedney Pickle Company in nearby Chaska. Did someone say diversification? In what had to be a first for a company whose stock in trade had been churches, schools, office buildings, and warehouses, Simons and his colleagues now had to learn about the chemical components of vinegar and brine and what such corrosive agents could do to steel and concrete.

"I was given a tremendous amount of responsibility, even though I had a lot to learn," Simons—named the firm's vice president at the age of twenty-six—would say later.

By the middle sixties, Gerry was himself only in his middle thirties, yet already becoming a formidable player in the regional construction and development industry. Always quietly confident, he'd nonetheless be surprised, during those early years, to find himself in a boardroom with the likes of some of the area's most prominent business leaders. "For a little guy off the farm like me to be hobnobbing with these big-time executives was really something, I'd think," he says. "But then they were all so friendly and nice, even to a little guy like me—that would surprise me, too!" He would be forever grateful for the older men's many kindnesses—and for the invaluable instruction they gave him, through word and example, in building and running a successful business.

That particular learning process started early.

"When I first started in business," Gerry says, "I opened my first checking account at the Bloomington-Richfield branch of Northwestern Bank then located in a trailer house at the corner of 78th Street and Penn. In 1960, I was invited to join the board of that branch. I joined that board and kept my business there for a number of years.

"One day I got a call from Henry Rutledge, who was president and CEO of the bank's holding company, asking if he could come out and visit me at my office. I thought, 'Wow, that's something. Here's the president of the largest bank in town asking if he can drop by for a visit!' Well, he came out and we sat down, and he asked me how I thought things were going at my branch. I told him that the branch president was a nice guy but had a serious drinking problem. Of course, Henry knew that already, but he was interested in knowing what I thought he should do about it. I said, 'I don't think you have a choice.' And, a short time later, the branch president was terminated. Now, as it turned out, the guy sobered up and turned his life around, so that was probably the best thing that could have happened to him. And I believe Henry appreciated my candor, my telling him exactly what I thought." Gerry and Rutledge became good friends, and Rutledge was one of Gerry's most important mentors over the years.

There would, to be sure, be many other mentors—and, again, with seemingly increasing frequency, one association and opportunity would lead to others.

"Patrick Butler was chairman of a fund drive at St. Thomas, and I was one of his vice chairs," Gerry recalls. "One day, after a meeting in Jim Shannon's office, Butler told me he was establishing a home for alcoholics up at Center City. Daniel Fourre was going to be the architect, but he wanted me to build it. Well, it turned out that what he had in mind would be the first building of the Hazelden Foundation."

Some time after that, Butler, who was on the board of the First National Bank of St. Paul, introduced Gerry to the bank's president, Clarence Frame. "I told Clarence that I was happy with Northwestern," Gerry says, "and he said, 'That's O.K., just come around sometime for a visit.' Which I did. We had a nice chat, and it was clear that Clarence was a nice, smart guy, but still, I was happy banking where I was and said so. Clarence replied, 'That's fine, but if you ever need anything, let me know.'

"Well, a couple of years after we built that first Howard Johnson's in Bloomington, the place was so successful that we wanted to build a fifty-room addition. We went to Northwestern Mutual Life, which had done the original financing, and told them we needed an increase in the mortgage. But NWML, which had us over a barrel in this situation, was going to require a big increase in the interest rate, which I didn't appreciate. So I thought about what Clarence had said to me when I'd met him. I called on him and said I needed a million dollars. And he said, 'O.K.' So then I went back to our man at NWML, and when he said either pay off the loan or pay the higher interest, I pulled Clarence's check out of my pocket and handed it to him. Needless to say, he was stunned. As for Clarence, when I suggested we document that million-dollar loan, he just said, 'No, that's all right. Just give me a letter saying you won't sell the Howard Johnson's to anybody.' Which was the way Clarence operated, and, in fact, the way a lot of good people used to do business around here."

Frame became a close friend and another valued mentor. And, when Gerry decided, in 1970, to add the first outsider to *his* board, the banker was the first person he asked. (Frame accepted and served on Gerry's board until he died in 1997.)

Gerry eventually joined, at Henry Rutledge's invitation, the Norwest Bank Corporation board. "By that time, I was forty-three years old," Gerry says. "At my first meeting I met a fellow named Bill Hodder, who, at forty, was the president of Target [then the fast-growing subsidiary of Dayton Hudson]. The two of us were brought in and introduced at the same time. I remember walking around the table, shaking hands with Mr. Pillsbury, Mr. Dayton, Mr. Bemis—all the big business names in town. Afterward I checked: The next youngest member of that board was fifty-eight. Somebody had obviously pounded on the table and said, 'We've got to get some youth in here!' And that turned out to be Bill and me."

Gerry was, in any event, an eager and adept learner. He was, those older businessmen would readily acknowledge, honest and smart. He stayed focused and worked hard.

"I never put a lot of pressure on myself," Gerry says of those formative years. "If I was going to make an important presentation, I'd make sure I was well-prepared, I'd speak to my God, and I'd tell myself, 'Just do the best you can. It's not the end of the world if you don't get what you want.' I'd tell myself to think, and go slow, 'and, when you say something, make sure it matters.' Back on the farm, my mother used to tell us, 'It's an empty barrel that makes the most noise.' So I reminded myself to not be an empty barrel. I also knew early on not to try to bluff something if I didn't know what I was talking about. I had learned that when I was teaching at Marquette. If someone asked me something I wasn't sure of, I'd say, 'I don't know the answer to that, but I will find out and get back to you.' People—whether they're your students or other businessmen—would respect your honesty."

In social settings—not an uncommon or unimportant part of doing business, he also learned early—Gerry had another exceptional asset in Hanky. Open and friendly but never a backslapper, Gerry would be pleased to have pretty, smiling Hanky—ever gracious and always knowing the right thing to say—at his side at business-related parties and receptions. "She just had a way about her," Gerry explains. On somber occasions, such as wakes and funerals, Gerry was inevitably uncomfortable and at a loss for the right words; fortunately, Hanky, whom he positioned in front of him when greeting the bereaved, never failed to offer the appropriately consoling comment.

Always, in every setting, Gerry says, "everybody was happy to see Hanky."

Building Strength, Inside and Out

With Gerry's increasing visibility and contacts within the metropolitan business community, the opportunities continued to rise in front of him. As was increasingly the case, his reputation preceded him.

While Normandale Industrial Park was taking form on the refurbished peatlands of Bloomington [according to Pine and Mundale], a second project with financial promise emerged in the same area. Ed Dunn and James Curry, partners in Dunn and Curry Insurance, were looking for better office facilities to house their growing agency. A client who had just moved into a brand-new building in Rauenhorst's Normandale Park told them about the leasing arrangements he and the construction company had made. "Rauenhorst put up the building," Dunn was told. "We pay rent, and at the end of fifteen or twenty years, if we like the building, we can buy it."

This was exactly the kind of arrangement Dunn was looking for. He made an appointment to see Gerry. He told him about the kind of building his agency needed, but he admitted that they were short of cash. "But we do own two farms in Bloomington that belonged to Curry's family," he said. Rauenhorst and Dunn drove out to the site overlooking the Minnesota River Valley. Within a few weeks they had made a deal: Dunn and Curry traded half their farmland for four acres of Normandale Park and an interest in a building Rauenhorst would construct on that acreage.

That 10,000-square-foot building at 4820 West 77th Street became the first unit of Pentagon Park, an office complex developed by Dunn and Curry and built by Rauenhorst Construction. Dunn and Curry planned to occupy half of their building and lease the other half. Within two months, however, they had filled the entire building and were making plans to construct a second.

Its buildings were not five-sided, but the name *Pentagon* Office Park stuck. Dunn and Curry had little reason to worry about finding tenants. Each building was fully leased before it was finished. The insurance agents turned developers made plans for more. By 1969, when Pentagon Park was completed, it covered more than sixty acres and contained twenty-one buildings, including a six-story tower. Rauenhorst Corporation had built it all.

Pentagon Park was not without its special demands, which made Gerry's business life at the time not only profitable but challenging.

"When we built the office tower there," Gerry explains, "our tests showed a layer of what's called 'fatty clay' about twenty feet underground. That meant that when you'd add the weight of the building, that clay way down there would compress and the building would sink. The obvious alternatives were to dig a tremendous hole and haul the clay out or drive pilings, both of which would have been very expensive.

"But I remembered, from my days at Marquette, that Miller Brewing Company had built a bottle house that, because of its tremendous weight, required they pour a solid footing about four feet deep under the entire building. So I engineered the same sort of thing for the tower at Pentagon Park. We designed a footing, three to four feet deep, with heavy reinforcing, so if the fatty clay settled, the building wasn't going to go anyplace.

"The day we installed it, we hired the entire output of three nearby Ready-Mix plants. We started work in the dark that morning and finished about three o'clock that afternoon, pouring continuously. We'd back one of the Ready-Mix trucks up to the site, open the chute, then send it back to the plant for another load. All told, we probably used about 1,600 cubic yards of concrete. But that was still more economical than digging out the clay or driving pilings. And that may have been the only building we ever built that, to the best of my knowledge, never had a crack in it!"

Gerry's reputation as an employer, meanwhile, was strengthening his operation from the inside out. Unlike *his* employers when he first entered the business out of college, he was known from the start as a fair, honest, and caring man for whom to work. Many of his employees, including early associates like Marcel Sciez, George Connor, and Nick Simons, stayed with him for decades. So did many of his supervisors and field people.

In 1994, Connor told an interviewer:

> Gerry's been able to command a loyalty that I've never seen anybody else command. We sort of kid among ourselves as having that Rauenhorst symbol on our backside! I think that's pretty much true throughout the organization.
>
> You can judge a man by how he treats some guy that's out in the cold pouring cement at ten below zero. And those guys love Gerry. They just do. Superintendents can go any place. They're skilled construction workers, and they've all stuck here. And they all speak well of Gerry.
>
> Gerry personally goes out and hands out hams at Christmas, and he's been doing that for years. He goes around to all the construction sites and makes sure everybody gets a ham. He treats his people right and has that personal touch.

In the early days, the relationship between Gerry and his employees was, as Connor put it, "a small, intimate sort of thing." Longtime employees would fondly remember lunch hours at Rauenhorst Construction, for instance. Individual brown bags gave way, early on, to a sort of communal kitchen in which everybody took his or her turn heating up the soup or lasagna, and that in turn gave way to a hired cook who created full-course meals for everyone. The point was a culture of personal connectedness and communication that proved at least as important as the meal itself.

Connor continued:

> We used to eat lunch together at the office, and that's, in a way,

what got us all so close. We'd all sit around the lunch table and talk. To this day, our lawyers, for instance, are able to talk to our engineers, draftsmen, architects, project managers, anybody. That was part of the culture that Gerry established here and that's been in place at least since I became involved in 1957.

The loyalty that employees felt for Gerry was reciprocated. Gerry was brought up to judge a person by the quality of his character; as an employer, he looked closely, in addition, at a person's skill and capacity for hard work. Creed and color were not factors to be considered in either hiring, job assignment, or promotion.

One of the company's early employees was an African-American named Al Willes. At the time, in the early 1960s, African-Americans were not common in the local building trades. "When Al came out and asked for a job, we hired him," Gerry recalls. "He was a good guy and a skilled worker, and everybody liked him. Well, one day he was laying bricks at one of our projects when some guys came up and said, 'You can't hire a black.' Our guys said, 'Why not?' And they said, 'You just can't. You've got to get rid of him.' We said, 'No, he's staying with us.' And he did." In fact, Willes stayed with the company for more than twenty years.

As important as his Catholicism was to him, Gerry refused to discriminate against people of other faiths among subcontractors and suppliers, either. "Some people might have thought they had an 'in' with us because they were Catholics, but that was never the case," he says. "Everybody who did business with us was evaluated according to the same criteria of price and performance, which I always felt was the only way to do business."

Always his own man himself, Gerry has always been partial, however, to independent operators. "We've always used ITOs—independent truck operators," he says, by way of example. "To this day, we use a lot of ITOs, in both our construction business and our concrete business. They're always on time, always in good shape, and always take good care of their trucks. I believe they're a great example of free enterprise."

"A Creative Work"

"I have always tried to do the best I could, and then accept the results," Gerry once told a reporter.

"People often ask about things like goals and objectives and budgets," he went on. "But I've always approached my work as though I were a football coach. You don't budget the score of a football game—you concentrate on doing the fundamentals well. It's the same in business. You look to the fundamentals—to basic, sound principles—and then you execute. Whatever the score is, it's a measure of your abilities."

By the mid-1960s, Rauenhorst Construction was very effectively executing the fundamentals, and the score, whether Gerry was carefully keeping track or not, was beginning to climb. At the end of 1963—that is, after the company's first decade in business—its annual construction volume totaled $6.5 million and about 175 people were on the payroll. Rauenhorst Construction had completed more than 210 projects, and those projects ranged from churches, schools, and office complexes to pickle factories, clubhouses, and hotels.

More significant change was in the works—and, in fact, change would become a constant in the company's development. That change, moreover, would, before too long, include the company's increasingly public identity.

As has been noted, Gerry originally called the firm Trojan Construction, after the family seed business. Then, however, he happened to have a chat with a colorful local businessman (and later state supreme court judge) named Peter Popovich, who asked him why he didn't use his own name as the company handle. "Nobody forgets *Popovich* when they hear it," Popovich told the younger man. "*Rauenhorst* is the same kind of name. It's a good, strong, unusual name. Nobody who hears it will forget it." So Gerry changed the name to Rauenhorst Construction. Then, in 1965, Gerry changed the name to Rauenhorst Corporation, which he felt better reflected the broader scope of the firm's activities at the time. A year later, the company adopted the distinctive dark-blue hexagonal logo.

With the company's increasing success in the sixties and seventies, however, came the concern that the memorable family name might become too visible for the family's good. "Hanky was all for changing the firm's name again," Gerry says. "She was mainly afraid of the kids being singled out at school and elsewhere. But I was afraid that changing the name would slow down our growth. People were beginning to know who we were by that time, and I believed that that identity was important. Finally, I suggested we let the kids themselves decide." Third child and second son Neil believed they should keep the family name on the corporate letterhead, but he and his dad were in the minority. The others—there were seven Rauenhorst children by that time—seemed to think a change would be wise.

Gerry, a stubborn man, was still not convinced. He sought out and polled the bearers of several well-known names in the community, including Kenneth Dayton of the department store dynasty and Harry Piper of the Piper Jaffray stock brokerage, none of whom endorsed a name change. "I still remember that lunch with Piper," Gerry says. "This was *after* his wife had been kidnapped [and later found unharmed], yet he said he'd never thought of changing his company's name."

Still, Hanky had the votes that counted—a majority of the immediate family. Robert Worthington, who was then a company planner, had suggested the name *Opus* for a pair of industrial parks under consideration at the time—the term is Latin for "a creative work"—and someone thought it would work well for the corporation itself. The name, and its meaning, had an undeniable appeal, and Gerry approved the formal change to Opus Corporation in 1982.

"*Opus* has worked out really well for us," he said recently. "It's fit us very well — and it's easy to remember. It's great for advertising, too. We put one of those big semi-trailers we use for tools and so forth at a construction site, and people can see those four big letters printed about seven feet tall on the side about a mile and a half away!"

All things considered, the young man who figured there had to be better ways of building and operating a business was finding those better ways in every part of his creation.

Chapter Three

Family

By most accounts, including his own, Gerry was as eager to start a family as he was to run his own business.

Of course, in the case of family, he wasn't thinking there had to be a better way. Why should he? He had grown up in a large, loving, supportive family whose collective strengths had overcome hard luck and the Great Depression. Like Hanky, moreover, Gerry had been raised in the Catholic faith, believing that family was sacred and that a child was a gift from God.

For that matter, the way he and Hanky viewed the world, family was second only to God himself—even more important than the business he was struggling to build—on their list of life's priorities.

Partners for Life

Hanky was Gerry's confidant and soul mate from the beginning, his closest friend, and his partner in both family and business. Indeed, when asked, during the company's fiftieth anniversary celebration, what he would do differently if he "had it to do all over again," he said there was really only one thing: "I would marry my wife sooner than I did."

When he came home discouraged from his first two jobs after college, Hanky listened sympathetically to his frustrations and dreams, and made it clear that she would accept whatever he decided to do with his career.

When he said, "I want to start my own business—will you help me?" she didn't hesitate. "Sure I will," she replied. Five decades later, when asked if she felt any trepidation at the time, she said, "I was never worried because *he* was so confident. He always looked on the bright side, and that confidence was infectious." And so, with her unstinting support, the business began.

Hanky's background, similar as it was in its positive details to Gerry's, and the many domestic skills she had learned as a girl, had prepared her well for a family of her own. As one of three daughters on her parents' farm, she had grown up preparing hearty meals for her father and his helpers. She was, in addition, a college graduate in her own right, whose brief but intensive experience as a home economist polished the "people skills" she would bring to her husband's business. Right out of college, she had worked as a customer service representative at Northern States Power Company in Minneapolis, responding to customer queries and often making home visits to find out why a homemaker's oven wasn't properly baking a cake. Still, she and Gerry both knew from the beginning that they would have as many children as God would give them and that she would stay home and take care of them. Thus, Judy's arrival in 1951, followed, in 1953, by Mark's effectively transformed Hanky into a part-time home-office manager and full-time at-home mom. It was a role she loved—and one at which she would obviously excel.

In the first few years of the business, Hanky would tend to her growing brood—eventually including Neil, who arrived in 1954, Joseph in 1956, and Michael in 1957—then help Gerry with his paperwork and other office tasks. "After I'd put the kids to bed in the evening, I would sit down at the typewriter and type his letters and get the mail ready for the next day and maybe do a little figuring, too, if it was needed," she recalled later. She'd catch up on her own diminished sleep by snatching a few winks when the children napped in the afternoon. (By the time children numbers six and seven—Susan and Amy—were born, in 1962 and 1964, respectively, the business had long since been physically removed from the home and Hanky had relinquished her office duties entirely.)

As many hours as Gerry put in on the job, he and Hanky made their evening meal together a lifelong habit. He would come home from work at suppertime, sit down with Hanky and the kids, take the aforementioned snooze, then work on his bids and other details until the wee hours of the next morning. The children became accustomed to the sanctity of the family supper, knowing that they could count on it as the one time of day when they would be certain to see their busy father and be together as a family. And it was Hanky who organized, prepared, and served that supper.

"I always saw her being the support for Dad," says Judy Rauenhorst Mahoney, the couple's first-born. "She was always home, keeping the family together, playing the traditional role of the wife of the fifties and sixties. She was always very interested in the business, but careful not to let the business overwhelm the family's concerns. Even at the dinner table, she was careful to make sure that not *too* much discussion was about company matters."

Son Michael recalls early company board member Clarence Frame saying of Hanky, "She was a reminder that this business was in it for the long haul and that its reputation was to be very carefully watched." Frame also remembered, says Michael, that Hanky always managed to find time to prepare cookies, cake, or pie for board meetings. (Hanky smiled when reminded of this years later, then said with typical self-deprecation, "Sometimes, if I was too busy at home, I'd use a boxed cake mix, but the men didn't seem to mind.") Michael adds: "When the business still operated out of the home, Mom would often prepare a little lunch or dessert for whomever might be there working or visiting. When the business moved out of the house, she frequently stopped by the office with a lunch or a plate of dessert."

Gerry will never be accused of excess in his personal tastes, but to the extent that, as the business became more and more successful, he was drawn to expensive cars, the latest in electronic gadgetry, and various domestic comforts, Hanky also functioned as a conservative counterforce. "There's no question we could have had bigger houses," Gerry once remarked, "but that's not what Hanky wanted. She's always liked nice things, and had an excellent eye for art and décor, but she didn't want to be ostentatious." Hanky's insistence on a low public profile was evident, as noted in the previous chapter, in her desire to change the corporate name from *Rauenhorst* to *Opus*. "It was Hanky who pushed that," says Gerry. But that was many years into their marriage. From the very beginning of their life together, her approach had been: *Make do with what you have. Don't put on airs. Don't boast about your possessions or accomplishments. Don't show off.*

Not that Gerry was ever, or became, with wealth, any more a spend-thrift than Hanky. Neither partner ever forgot the lessons learned growing up during the Depression. "That carefulness with money is ingrained in you when you grow up not having much," Hanky explains. "When you're raised like that, you're just not comfortable paying twice as much as you may think something's worth, even if you now have the money to do it."

Theirs wasn't the kind of relationship that encouraged secrets. Gerry would tell Hanky what was happening on the job, and much of that information, provided it wasn't sensitive or confidential, would be shared with the kids. In the company's first few years, Gerry would have his crew chiefs come over to the house on Thursday nights for their weekly meetings. Hanky would shush the kids out of the living room where the men sat discussing their work, but the kids would inevitably wander back and say hello. That seemed fine with the visitors—most of whom were family men themselves—and the experience would give the kids a sense of being part of their dad's work in a way that a lot of other kids (and their dads) could only envy. It was truly, and from the start, a *family* business.

"My first memories," Judy recalls, "are of all those construction people coming and going to and from our little house on 18th Avenue in Rich-field. And I remember one of the first trucks Dad bought—how proud he was of that truck." Judy also remembers her father conducting business out of the Gerry-built breezeway. "It was a very small space," she says. "Just room enough for a desk and chair."

The first year or two on his own, Gerry worked seven days most weeks—

that's just what entrepreneurs starting their own businesses seemed to do. Later he would observe: "It's easy to become a workaholic, especially when you like what you do." Then, one day, one of Hanky's relatives stopped by to say hello while the man's daughter was undergoing rehabilitation for polio at the Sister Kenny Institute in Minneapolis. The man was a farmer, and it was April—prime planting time—but there he was, on a Sunday afternoon, a long way from the farm.

Gerry said, "Gee, how can you take off like this? Everybody must be planting."

To which the farmer replied, "If I can't make a living in six days, I sure as heck won't do it in seven."

From that point on, Gerry didn't work on Sunday—no matter how busy he was (or wanted to be). Sunday became Family Day, no matter what. And Gerry, decades later, says he believes that seventh day away from business was as good for him as it was for his appreciative wife and kids. In any case, wherever they were living and whatever the status of the business, he and Hanky and the children would dutifully troop off to church on Sunday morning. Mass would be followed by one of Hanky's excellent, farm-style dinners. Then parents and kids would pile into the family car for an afternoon jaunt for ice cream and a visit to one or more of Dad's projects.

"Sometimes, when Judy was still really little, we'd drive over to one of the city lakes for a picnic," Gerry recalls. "As the kids got older, we'd visit our families. Hanky's sister lived nearby, and her kids were about the same age as ours. We'd also drive out to Olivia, where we still had a lot of relatives."

Most important, the burgeoning family had quality time together and the kids could see first-hand what their father did all day and much of the evening during the rest of the week.

Construction Projects and Popsicle Sticks

Unlike the fathers of most of their friends, the Rauenhorst kids' dad built things they could see, touch, smell, walk around, climb up into, climb down out of, watch grow, and otherwise investigate.

"That was probably the best part of it," son Neil recalls. "That it was tangible. We could go see it, walk through it...." Eventually, there was also the property their father was holding, often undeveloped suburban land, sometimes with quarries or gravel pits to explore. After Gerry moved the company into its own building, and as the children grew older, Gerry would bring them to the office, or to construction sites, allowing them to "help out" while he worked.

"I got in the habit of taking one of the kids with me every Saturday," Gerry explains. "We'd go to the office, and there'd be nobody else there, so it would be a good time for me to get a lot of work done. I'd take one kid at a time, sort of rotate. He or she could play with the typewriter or the calculator, and ask me this or that. That way I got to spend a lot of time with the family even when I was working all the time, and it got them involved in the business. They grew up knowing what was going on. They grew up knowing what I did all day."

"One of my favorite memories is of testing the new concrete floor in one of Dad's buildings with our roller skates," Judy told an interviewer. "After the concrete had dried, we would be the first people on it—and we could roller-skate through the whole building."

Judy continued: "One summer Dad said we could have all the Popsicles we wanted—but we had to save the sticks. So every time the ice cream truck came by, Mom let us go out and buy Popsicles. We put the sticks in a box, and at the end of the summer Dad designed a roof using the Popsicle sticks and Elmer's Glue. It was the model for the roof of the Normandale Golf Course building."

"One of my first memories was stopping by a construction site Dad had to look at when I was very little," says Mark. "I remember from way back how hard he tried to include us in what he was doing. I remember going with him when I was really young, looking at sites and sometimes sitting on the construction equipment, which was very exciting. I remember the men coming over at night for meetings and hearing my father talking business on the phone in the breezeway of that first house, but it wasn't until I started going out with him to the sites that I really began to get a sense of what he actually did for a living.

"As we got older and could understand more, he loved to explain things to us—the way something was built or why he used such and such a wall system, for example. He obviously had his heart in his work, that was always evident. But then he always has his heart in what he's doing—or else he doesn't do it."

"We were exposed to the business very early," says Neil. "My earliest memories are those of going to the office on Saturdays and then driving around with my father looking at the various projects. We talked about the projects we'd look at, and we talked about all kinds of things relating to the projects and the business. As a young boy, I was very interested in all of that."

The company was still relatively small at the time, and there was little indication, at least as far as the children were concerned, that it was going to get appreciably larger. Neil recalls a road trip the family took out West one summer in the early sixties. Somewhere en route they stopped and toured a large paper factory. "At one point the guy giving us the tour said they had more than a thousand people working at the plant," Neil says. "I remember turning to my father and asking, 'Dad, do you think your company will ever be that big?' And Dad immediately and matter-of-factly replied, 'No, I don't think so.'"

Which isn't to say, however, that their father didn't have bigger things in mind behind the modest demeanor. "Our dinner-table discussions with Dad were about building projects that started as 'small acorns,'" says Michael. "But those projects were usually located, designed, and financed so that they would grow into the 'oaks' they are today. We all became familiar with those projects, and, as we grew older, he sometimes used us as a sounding board."

For the most part, though, it was difficult for Gerry's kids to separate the business from fun. Says Joe:

> I remember my father would take me down to the office on Saturday mornings. By that time, the company was headquartered at 4444 Rauenhorst Circle in Bloomington. I remember running

around the office, looking at everything, and he always had a whole bunch of neat gadgets and what we thought of at the time as a hidden bathroom. (Actually, the door was built into the wood paneling and thus was easily imagined by a kid to be "invisible.") He had little things—hidden buttons in the carpet—that you pushed on to open and close the drapes. He had a calculator on his desk that was the size of a small refrigerator. Actually, it was an early computer, though it was basically a calculator, and he was one of the first to have one. He also had a car phone before hardly anyone had a car phone. It was a mobile phone. There was always that fascination with gadgets.

I also remember going to job sites. My father would take me through a new office building and point out things he thought I should see. I would ask question after question, which he would answer patiently. He was always very willing to let us know what was going on in the business.

Susan Rauenhorst Turner, the sixth of the seven Rauenhorst children, says:

One of my first recollections as a little girl was sitting around the dinner table, discussing how Dad's day was. He was always home for dinner and always with the family when he was home at that time. The focal point at the dinner table would be how his day was, then we'd go into everybody else's day. Dad worked on Saturday, but he would always take one or more of us with him.

I remember as a little kid, at St. Richard's grade school in Richfield, the other kids would tell me that my dad built this building or my dad built that building, and I thought, "Isn't that what *every* dad does?"

For a while our parents would rent a room on the pool level at the Howard Johnson's Dad owned in Bloomington, and, as a special treat, we'd go there and swim on a weekend. Someone would say, "Dad built this," and I'd just think, "O.K.," like it wasn't unusual, that that's what dads did.

Amy and I were always "the little girls" because Michael, the next oldest, is four years older than I am. So Amy and I were always dressed in matching dresses and tagged along with the others. I remember going to the gravel pit off France Avenue, when Dad's office was on Rauenhorst Circle. Everybody at the office was so nice—and many of those employees are still with the company today! It was always a family oriented atmosphere.

Business and family have always been entwined. The family values are in the business, and the business values are part of the family. That has affected our work ethic and the way we treated other people and expected to be treated and how we were expected to do things honestly and fairly.

"I remember telling my friends and classmates, '*My* daddy builds buildings!'" Amy Rauenhorst Goldman, the youngest of Gerry and Hanky's children, says. "To me, Dad's always been larger than life, charismatic, inspiring. We knew what he did for a living, and we were all so proud of him. He was someone we idealized. We all wanted his approval."

Logically enough, given the children's early and extensive exposure to their father's business, the company became a source of weekend and summer jobs. Nobody, by the way, was allowed to loaf in this family, even after the company became successful and, eventually, *hugely* successful. Money wasn't the point. According to Gerry and Hanky, honest work was a gift from God, too, and nobody would be permitted to ride on the industry of others.

An early company history recorded the first jobs of the oldest Rauenhorst kids, which would be typical of those that followed:

Mark watered the shrubbery around the firm's [first] headquarters on Fremont Avenue. He had to do it right—train the hose on the brick wall rather than on the dirt around the plants.

There would be no mud splatters on the exterior of the Rauenhorst building.

As a thirteen-year-old, Mark spent his Christmas vacation repairing electrical cords in the construction shop. He continued in the shop the next summer, repairing equipment, doing inventory, washing cars. Even then, he knew he had a special responsibility as the boss's son. "From day one," he recalls, "Dad told me that if he was going to give me that job, I had to perform, to set an example. I took it very seriously. Now I know it was his way of helping me internalize the work ethic that is so important to him."

Neil's first summer jobs were washing cars and cleaning construction equipment as it came in from the field. But his interest in architecture surfaced early, and by the time he was in high school, he was helping the company's staff architects construct models of buildings—Normandale Industrial Park, Northwestern Financial Center.

Judy created the company's first newsletter as a high school student. Called the *Rauenhorst Roundup*, it contained articles about construction projects. Judy wrote, took photographs, and helped produce and distribute the newsletter.

(Mostly) Happy Memories

Of course, life in the Rauenhorst home wasn't all about business. The kids all attended Catholic schools, ran around with neighborhood playmates, took part in sports, ballet, and other childhood enthusiasms, and generally enjoyed the comfortable lifestyle of an up-and-coming suburban family that was common enough in post-war America.

There were also the funny, random, quirky things that they would be able to recreate in their mind's eye the rest of their lives.

For Judy, those memories include their gadget-happy father installing the first automatic garage-door opener in their Richfield neighborhood. "My dad was on the leading edge of technology," she says, laughing at the recollection. "But that house was very close to the airport, and the garage-door device was apparently on the same radio frequency as the planes flying low overhead, so in the middle of the night we'd hear the garage door going up and down, up and down!"

Mark recalls Gerry napping on the living room couch while Hanky reminded the kids to play quietly because their dad "really needed his sleep." Mark also has indelible images of his father, early in the company's life, religiously reading the newspaper before going off to work in the morning and signing payroll checks on Thursday evening.

All of the kids talk about the frequent appearance in their childhood home of various priests and bishops. More often than not, the clerics were familiar and revered faces from the local parish or archdiocese; every once in a while, however, there was a more exotic guest, such as Archbishop Harold Henry, who would update the Rauenhorsts on his mission work that the Rauenhorsts were helping support in Korea.

(Harold Henry was a priest of the Columban Mission Society born and raised in Northfield, Minnesota. Over the course of a long and storied career, he was a prisoner of the Japanese, a front-line chaplain during World War II, and later an enemy of the Communist government of North Korea. More important, after a total of forty-two years in Korea, he had built forty-six churches, a hospital, three clinics, several leper colonies, nine high schools, and a seminary. The Rauenhorsts met him at a reception in Minneapolis for Bishop Fulton J. Sheen, the renowned television personality. Gerry casually suggested that Henry "drop by the house sometime"—and the next day Henry appeared at the family's front door. The archbishop and the Rauenhorsts remained close friends—visiting each other in America and Korea as frequently as possible—until his death in 1976.)

"Archbishop Henry taught poor Korean families about raising pigs and would give a family twelve piglets on condition that they pay him back with twelve more piglets," Michael recalls. "I grew up hearing stories like that, and it ended up changing my life."

"A lot of those priests I considered uncles," Susan says. "They were at our home so often it really didn't seem unusual at the time. It was only later, when I was older, that I really began to understand how fortunate we were to get to know them as well as we did. And I think a lot of their influence has filtered down into the philanthropic work we've been involved with as adults. A lot of that comes, of course, from our folks, but the influence of those priests has played a large part, too."

Then there was the day the family was delivered from the potentially deadly havoc caused by the oil truck that crashed into the house.

That happened on an otherwise uneventful afternoon after Gerry had moved the company office out of the Richfield house and into the new building on Fremont Avenue. Hanky had just put baby Joe down for his nap and sat down at the kitchen table for a quick bite to eat. Suddenly, glancing out the window, she saw a large oil truck lurch out of control, leave the street, and hurtle toward the house. There was a tremendous noise, then an explosion of glass and plaster as the truck hit the house near the bedroom where moments earlier Hanky had laid Joe in his crib.

The side of the house was badly damaged, but, miraculously, Joe was untouched. In fact, when Hanky rushed into the room, he was sound asleep in his crib. The other children had either been out in the yard, away from the damage, or playing in another part of the house at the time, and were likewise unscathed. But Gerry, reached by phone at the office, rushed home and held his shaken family tight for several moments. It had been a close call, and, as he and Hanky saw it, their narrow escape from grievous harm was dramatic proof that God was watching over them.

In 1958, the family moved from that Richfield home to a larger house on a larger lot in Edina. Seventeen years later, they moved again, to a still larger house on still larger grounds in Edina. The family would eventually spend the lion's share of their summers in the beautiful Brainerd lakes area of northern Minnesota. When school let out in early June, Hanky and the kids would essentially resettle in a large cabin that Gerry and Hanky had bought in the fall of 1967. For twenty-five years, the cabin was the ideal lakeside getaway for the family. Then an unusual opportunity—to acquire a nearby setting that today comprises one hundred acres—presented itself. Gerry tells the story:

We originally had the land on the other side of the lake. We'd looked at [the current] space for a long time and asked the owner to let us know if and when she wanted to sell it. Finally, in 1988, the owner put it up for auction.

At the auction, there were about a dozen bidders. The property was to be bid in two sections, then in total. Now I'd been to a lot of auctions in my life. I'd also learned a lot about auctions from my brother Clete, who'd been to even more than I had. Hanky and I had talked about our plan in advance and at great length. We'd decided we wanted the land, but would stick to a maximum value, because it was so easy to get carried away at an auction.

Well, the bidding went on for an hour or two. Finally, there were only two of us going down the stretch—and we were bidding for the whole piece. The lawyer was standing on the steps of the cabin that was there then, and the two of us remaining bidders kept pushing the price up. Eventually we got to the maximum amount Hanky and I had agreed we wouldn't exceed. I looked at her and said, "That's it." But, God love her, she looked back at me and said in no uncertain terms, *"This is for the kids!"* So I upped my opponent on the next bid. He bid once more, then folded and went home. The property wasn't what we intended to pay for it, but it was ours—and our children's—and we've never regretted buying it for a moment.

More distant excursions—during summer vacations, holidays, and other breaks in the school year—also played an important part in the family's life almost from the beginning.

"When Judy was about nine or ten, we took our first big trip," Gerry recalls. "We had four kids with us. We'd made arrangements to drive a car for a dealer we knew to California. It was quite an event for us— something entirely new—having all those kids in the car for such a long trip." Soon enough, however, such trips became common, even though the destinations, and occasionally the mode of transport, were often out of the ordinary. "Every year there was that big family trip somewhere," Neil says. "The Black Hills, California, the East Coast, Canada, England, Germany...." There were also notable trips to the Far East, where family members visited Archbishop Henry's mission school in Seoul, and several visits to the Vatican, which sometimes included audiences with the Pope.

If Gerry could combine a little business with their pleasure, so much the better. In 1967, the family's big annual getaway featured a visit to the World's Fair in Montreal. The Rauenhorst itinerary included an unlikely stop in Grand Rapids, Michigan, where the family transferred to, and commenced the rest of the trip in, a Checker cab that had been custom-painted in the unmistakable orange and aqua colors of a Howard Johnson hotel (two of which Gerry then owned back in the Twin Cities). "It was an honest-to-goodness Checker taxi cab, with four seats and eight doors—so every kid had a door," Gerry says, still tickled at the thought of their unusual conveyance. "We were in heaven, driving from Grand Rapids to Montreal and then all the way back to Minneapolis. Then it became the official airport limo of our Bloomington hotel, and we eventually ran the tires off it." (The Checker was sold with the Bloomington HoJo in the late sixties.)

Later trips, which involved either all or individual members of the immediate family, included jaunts to other World's Fairs and the annual Super Bowl (in various locations) as well as hunting and fishing trips to wilderness areas in Canada and Alaska. For his sixteenth birthday, Gerry and Hanky gave Mark the gift of flying lessons, so Mark, who became an enthusiastic and accomplished pilot, eventually provided the transportation for the outdoor adventures.

Sometimes the trips included old friends of the family—and, occasionally, resulted in the making of new ones. In 1976, for instance, Gerry took Monsignor Terrence Murphy and the three youngest Rauenhorst kids to the Summer Olympics in Montreal. Gerry happened to have an extra ticket for the finals of the women's gymnastics competition, which that year starred fourteen-year-old sensation Nadia Comaneci of Rumania. Minneapolis entrepreneur, sports fan extraordinaire, and eventual best-selling author Harvey McKay was desperate for a ticket to the event, and Gerry gave him his extra. "Ever since, Harvey's been most accommodating when I've called him for a ticket—to the World Series, Super Bowl, or whatever," Gerry says. "Later on, when he told me he was going to write a book, I took $20 out of my pocket and said, 'Here. I just bought the first copy.' Some time after that, I ran into him at the airport and he autographed a copy of the book, reminding me that I had been his first sale."

Hanky, for her part, had an educated and discerning eye for fine art and antiques, so the family travels, especially to Europe and other ancient locations, frequently involved visits to both well-known museums and out-of-the-way galleries and shops. In later years, Gerry and Hanky would occasionally make carefully considered purchases of artworks and artifacts, such as a full suit of medieval armor (which Gerry once donned for a party), to grace the family home or be presented to one of the institutions the family was helping support.

Gerry, predictably, was attracted to the notable architecture of the sites they were touring, and often provided a running commentary on the subject of vaulted ceilings, flying buttresses, and other specifics for the benefit of his wife and children.

He recalls, for instance, an early visit to the Vatican with the children almost thirty years ago.

"We were walking around inside St. Peter's," he says. "We had just built the Northwestern Financial Center back home, twenty-four stories tall, and I said to the kids, 'That tower would fit inside this building!'

"Until you'd seen it, you couldn't possibly appreciate how big St. Peter's was. And to think they built it without tower cranes and the other machinery we take for granted today. I still think it's absolutely amazing."

The Second Generation at Opus

Clearly, their seven children have been Hanky and Gerry's pride and joy—and raising them their greatest and most fulfilling achievement.

They brought up their children, they've both been quick to explain, to live by the Golden Rule, the teachings of the Catholic church, and the common sense guidelines Hanky and Gerry had been brought up with—albeit while acknowledging that times and customs change. "I'd say we were moderately strict with the children," Hanky once said. "There were rules they had to abide by, but, at the same time, they've had a certain amount of freedom to enjoy themselves and find themselves as individuals. They've certainly had more freedom than *our* generation ever had!"

Hanky acknowledged that the circumstance of growing up with the affluence her children have enjoyed has created a challenge and obligation that *her* parents wouldn't have been able to imagine. "The Lord has certainly blessed us," she said, alluding to the family's current situation. "I have always felt that we return a lot in what we do [through philanthropy], and I hope we've instilled that sense in our children. It's a different world that we live in now than the one Gerry and I grew up in. Our families worked eighteen hours a day to survive through the Depression. We grew up with very little, so all this we have now is quite a gift. I have tried to instill in our children appreciation and respect for what we've been given."

Everybody agrees that the seven children were, from the start, seven individuals, with their own distinct personalities and interests and, eventually, their own, separate visions of their future. Gerry made no secret of his desire to see his kids follow him into the business. Just as his mother had encouraged her children to stick together on the family farm and in its seed-corn business, Gerry believed in the value—and values—of the family firm. It has troubled him deeply that modern America seems indifferent, even hostile in terms of its tax policies, to the concept of the multigenerational family business. He's long admired, by contrast, the famous European and Asian tradition of passing down a company's ownership from one generation to the next over the course of several centuries and a half-dozen or more generations.

Still, when his kids were in their formative stages, he understood human nature and the differences of personality, ability, and inclination, and he knew better than to push his offspring in directions that they might not wish, or be able, to go.

"Dad used to say, 'You will all decide for yourselves what you want to do,'" Mark Rauenhorst points out. "And, basically, as long as it was something we would do a good job at and be happy with, he gave us the impression that he would be happy with our choice as well. He wanted to see us find our own niche in life and be successful on our own.

"I think that, as much as he would have preferred it, he was careful about not over-promoting our joining the family business. Of course, he never discouraged it, either. I think he just wanted it to be an opportunity that we could take advantage of if we wanted to."

Joe says, "I was always interested in the family business because it was something I grew up in. Like my brothers and sisters, I learned a lot about Opus around the kitchen table. My father was always eager to talk about what he did that day. I know there are people who believe that you shouldn't talk business at the table, that you should leave the work at the office and concentrate on other things at home, but I found my father's talk about the business interesting and instructive.

"But I don't think I decided early on that I wanted to go into my father's business. I just knew that if I was interested and capable, some-day I *could*. I say *capable* because Gerry made it clear that in *this* family's business, you would get a job and then get ahead based on merit, not on being the son of the owner. That was very important. Everyone was the same in that regard. Your being offered a job and eventually the chance to advance would be predicated on merit. He may not have said it in so many words, but we all knew his philosophy regarding hard work and being productive and not getting any handouts."

But if Gerry could or would not pressure his kids to come into the business (provided, as Joe suggests, they are able), at least he could exert some influence on their choice of college or university prior to their starting a career. As Judy succinctly recounts her father's proposition: "We were told we could go to any college we wanted. But he would pay our tuition only if the college we chose was Catholic." Not surprisingly, each of the kids, in turn, chose a Catholic institution for their undergraduate studies—though, interestingly enough, no two chose the same. None chose their parents' Twin Cities alma maters, either, though Judy would earn her master's and Joe his bachelor's degree at Marquette.

(There was another "rule," too: If you complete your undergraduate studies in four years, you get a new car. "And what do you know?" Gerry says. "All seven of them finished in four years!")

Their respective courses of study and initial career choices varied significantly as well. Judy went off to St. Mary's, associated with the University of Notre Dame, in South Bend, Indiana, where she focused on humanistic studies and French. Mark attended Creighton, in Omaha, Nebraska, and majored in business and finance. Neil studied architecture at the Catholic University of America in Washington, D.C. From Marquette, Joe moved to the University of San Francisco to study law. Michael went to Notre Dame. Susan did her undergraduate work at Gonzaga University in Spokane. Amy attended Georgetown University in Washington, D.C. Each of the seven continued on to graduate school and earned at least one advanced degree.

Four of the kids—Mark, Judy, Neil, and Joe—worked for Opus after college. Each had to follow Gerry's rule requiring at least three years of productive employment with another company (in any industry) before joining the family firm.

Judy eventually joined Opus's marketing department and worked a "short year" before she "retired" to raise her own family. The mother of four grown or nearly grown children, she has since started her own highly successful language-education business, called *Teach Me Tapes*. Mark has risen to top management of the company since joining it in 1982. He became president in 1999 and also CEO in 2000. Neil worked at the prestigious Chicago architectural firm of Skidmore, Owings & Merrill for three years, then joined Opus's Chicago office (in the Real Estate Development Group) in 1982. In 1988, he became president of Opus South in Tampa, responsible for the company's southeastern U.S. operations. He left Opus in April 2002 to open his own development company in Tampa. Joe practiced law in San Francisco for eight years, becoming a partner in his firm, prior to being hired at Opus in 1989; he's now president of Opus South. Mike earned a law degree, worked for four years with refugees in Thailand, and now works for a Deutschebank development fund in New York. Susan and Amy, after earning advanced degrees and spending time in various professional and philanthropic pursuits, are full-time wives and mothers. All the kids stay in close touch with their parents and each other, and meet as a group at least twice a year to discuss common concerns.

Working in your father's business has always had its privileges. The affection and deference that other employees feel for the founder are often enjoyed by the offspring as well. But there are pressures as well. Special rules sometimes have to be established lest the family be accused, for example, of nepotism. "One ground rule in my case," Mark says, "was that my father never decided my pay. I worked directly for him for only a short time anyway. Most of the time I worked for somebody else. And even when I did work directly for my dad, Keith Bednarowski was my supervisor and decided what I earned. So we've always sort of kept our distance."

Sometimes the concerns are less weighty, but require adjustments as well. Joe notes, for instance: "I refer to Dad as *Gerry* because everybody around the company refers to him as *Gerry*. It makes some people there uncomfortable if I call him *Dad*. So I've just gotten into the habit of calling him by his first name like everybody else." (As it happens, Mark calls Gerry *Dad*. When asked which he prefers, Gerry replied, "I couldn't care less.")

From Gerry's point of view, adjusting the father-child relationship to one of founder/owner-employee/possible successor can be difficult, too. Gerry had Bob Dahlin, who was then Opus's president, work out the details of Mark coming to work for the company in 1982. He has also relied on Bednarowski, who joined the company as a project manager in 1969 and is now chairman of the board, to communicate with the second generation about any number of issues. Bednarowski, for his part, acknowledges his appointed role as a sort of non-family mentor to the Rauenhorst kids, but insists that Gerry has not lost, or yielded, any influence. "He still has tremendous influence on his children," Bednarowski says. "In different ways, but on all of his kids."

Bednarowski also seconds what many acquaintances, including Gerry's kids, have been saying for years: However you define the job or the situation, "Gerry is a tough act to follow."

Two Families, No Regrets

Looking at their father over the passing years, the seven siblings have come to appreciate aspects of his life and values that they wouldn't have understood as children. They all talk, for example, about his work ethic and his desire to do the right thing by his God, family, and community, and they suggest that the status and affluence generated by his business success was the byproduct, not the objective, of his finding all those better ways.

"I don't think he's ever been obsessed with money—with money for money's sake," Mark says. "I think his concern, early on, was security for his family. The struggle his parents endured, especially after they were driven off their land, had a profound effect on him. So, first, he was absolutely determined to make sure he could take care of his family. As time passed and he was obviously successful, the goal became more a matter of taking care of those in the larger community who were less fortunate than he was.

"As a kid, I remember his talking about people who had been successful, but saying that the money those people made was only a small piece of their success, the way he saw it. The important thing to him was doing it the right way, changing things for the better, and making a difference for the good. If the money followed, great. But that was not the goal. I never got the sense that making money was the driving force in my father's life."

"Dad was not entirely successful in preparing me for the family business," Michael says, half jokingly, "but he and Mom sure prepared me for the rest of the world. They did so much, as Mom would say, to 'broaden our horizons,' but what I cherish most are the roots they gave us. We did everything as a family. Even today, Mom and Dad's happiest moments are those they spend with the family.

"I'm also really quite in awe that after all Mom and Dad achieved, they have such a deep sense of compassion for those in need. They exemplify the phrase 'To whom much has been given, much will be expected in return.' Our parents taught us that while business matters are important, helping others was also a part of life and that personal service was the core of that."

In every aspect of their life together, the Rauenhorst children view their mother as their father's constant source of support and encouragement, always there for him and sometimes providing a function that might have surprised outsiders who saw her only in social situations. For instance, her children agree, she was a shrewd judge of character whom Gerry relied on when considering someone for an important job or promotion.

"My dad used my mom as a sounding board—always," Neil recalls. "Especially regarding personnel matters. And it was always quite apparent that her insight and judgment were remarkably acute. He'd tell me sometimes that when the company was smaller, he'd interview a prospective manager and go back and forth trying to decide what to do, and then he and Mother would have dinner with the prospect and in the car on the way home, she'd tell him what she thought of the guy. Dad knew he could count on that. She was a remarkable judge of character, and that was very valuable to him."

Hanky's influence on Gerry was readily apparent to observers outside the family, too.

Keith Bednarowski says: "I used to get Hanky's goat by referring to her as Gerry's boss. Gerry loved it when I said that. Hanky acted as though she didn't like my saying it, but I think secretly she did. At any rate, that's the impression I got when I'd see them together—that he would do anything she wanted. There's no question about one thing: She has been a *very* important part of his life, and he has been a very important part of hers. You couldn't ask for anything better than that, could you?"

To say that the Rauenhorsts have long shared the same wave length would be an obvious understatement. Consider the story Gerry loves to tell about a Pierce Arrow:

We bought a piece of land once from a guy down in Eagan. Turns out the guy had twenty antique autos in a storage shed on the property, that portion of which the state had condemned. So he auctioned off all but his three favorites: a 1917 Maxwell, a 1929 Packard, and a 1937 Pierce Arrow.

A few months later, he apparently needed some money so he called and asked if I wanted to buy the Packard, which I did.

A few months after that, he called and wanted to sell me the Pierce Arrow. I didn't have *that* much interest in vintage cars, so this time I said no. But the guy kept calling, until one day in December I thought, 'What the heck, I might as well buy it.' But when I called him back, he said, 'Gerry, you won't believe this, but a woman walked in here just this morning and bought the car.' So I forgot about it.

Then a few weeks later I was taking a nap on Christmas afternoon when Hanky and Mark woke me up. They took me down to the garage, and there was that thirty-seven Pierce Arrow, with the biggest red bow you've ever seen!

Then there's the sequel, which Gerry relates with equal relish.

A fellow was selling golf carts that were built to look like a 1932 Ford V-8. One day Hanky and I looked at one and thought it would be a nice thing to have at the lake. Several years later, I was wondering what to buy Hanky for Christmas. So I called the manufacturer and said I'd like to order one of those golf carts. I asked him to send me a photo of the cart so I could put it in Hanky's Christmas card. For some reason, the guy was hemming and hawing, but then he agreed to take care of it.

Well, Christmas comes and the family is opening presents. I open an envelope, and there's a photo of the same golf cart—with Christmas greetings from Hanky. We had given each other the same thing!

(After Christmas, the manufacturer called and asked if we wanted both carts. I said, "Thanks, but one will be enough.")

Hanky has said many times that she's never regretted not having a career of her own, despite her college training and her brief professional experience. "Once the children started coming along, I never could have handled both the child-rearing and a career, or I couldn't have done both jobs as well as I think they should have been done," she once explained. "Besides, our marriage and our family life has been so pleasant, so happy, I wouldn't have traded it for anything. I can honestly say I've had no second thoughts about the choices I've made."

Sister Andrea Lee, president of the College of St. Catherine, Hanky's alma mater, said recently, "I have no doubt whatsoever that had Henrietta continued her career in home economics, she would have been a huge success in her own right. However, she chose instead to become a partner with her husband and together they built a great corporation. And I'm convinced he couldn't have done that without her support, counsel, and total dedication.

"I've never met two people so completely in love who have partnered together to build a business on one hand and to raise seven beautiful, loving children on the other."

Hanky has occasionally thought about how different her life would have been if she had married a different farmer's son and stayed in Renville County, as many of her relatives and friends did. (That had been, in fact, a very real possibility following her father's sudden death of a heart attack while she was in college. She and her father had been exceptionally close, and she had often worked alongside him in the fields. Now, after he died, she seriously considered returning to the farm to help out and care for her mother. "In the end," says son Michael, "her two older sisters, Ciel and Margaret, agreed to look after their mom, so Hanky finished her degree and took that job in Minneapolis.") "Now and then one of my aunts would say, 'Now, Henrietta, did you ever think when you were a little girl that you would be doing what you're doing now that you're grown up and living in a big house in the city and going on those trips you take?'" Hanky has recalled. "And I'd always say, 'No, Aunt Marie, I never, *ever* thought that.'"

She would concede that there have been special duties and responsibilities she's had as the wife of a company founder and owner. "There was always a certain amount of entertaining," she's explained. "For instance, before the company got so big, we always had the annual Christmas party at our house. And in the summer we'd have a company picnic in a public park and invite all the families, and I would be in charge of that, too. Early on, it was my job to select the Christmas gifts we'd give at the party. But those were always wonderful, happy affairs, and I enjoyed that part of my life as well."

She and Gerry have worked hard to stay in touch with friends and acquaintances from the old days, when the company was small enough for them to know everybody, everybody's spouse, and everybody's children, too, on a first-name basis. "Our Christmas card list hasn't changed a lot," Hanky remarked a few years ago. "We've continued to be friends with a lot of the same people we've been friends with for years, *decades* in many cases. To me, that says we haven't changed a lot over the years, that our values haven't changed, even though our circumstances have. I'm always pleased when somebody says, 'Oh, you two haven't changed at all!'"

"I have two families," Gerry has long been fond of saying. "My own family and my Opus family." Many observers might say that, in truth, those two families have been one.

Chapter Four

Faith

One of Gerry Rauenhorst's favorite quotations comes from the teachings of St. Augustine: "I shall work as if everything depended on me, I shall pray as if everything depended on God."

If there was ever a succinct description of the division of labor in one man's life, that might be it.

Hard work and steady prayer are the paired wheels that have taken Gerry from his hardscrabble youth on a tenant farm to the unimagined success and status he enjoys today. The work and prayer have been conflated in the rockribbed Catholic faith that has guided Gerry and Hanky through their roughly parallel childhoods and education, their courtship and marriage, and finally their long, fruitful partnership as parents and grandparents.

As everyone who knows them will attest, the Rauenhorsts have lived their faith every day of their lives.

And, to this day, the Rauenhorsts themselves will aver, nothing in their lives is more important.

A Living, Giving Faith

Gerry did not come to his faith as, say, Augustine did. The children of Henry and Margaret Rauenhorst were *born* to it—or, rather, *in* it, the way a fish is born in water. Gerry's is as natural, as unself-conscious, a faith as friends and acquaintances say they've ever seen. They say his faith is as much a part of him as his brown eyes and easy smile.

His earliest memories include regular visits to St. Aloysius, the Catholic church in Olivia. The Rauenhorsts had been practicing Catholics for generations, long before they came to this country. In Olivia, St. Aloysius reflected the several ethnic heritages of the community. "Our church was half Bohemian," Gerry recalls, referring to the large Czech population in that part of western Minnesota. "The pastor, Father Henry Pomije, was Bohemian and multilingual, and preached in English and Bohemian, except on Christmas and Easter, when he preached in English, Bohemian, and *German*. He was very autocratic, our pastor, and he built that big, beautiful church, with granite and marble and a big tower, back in 1929. I remember my mother saying what a good—but also what a strong and tough—man he was.

"The church had a pair of double doors in front and a door on each side. On Sunday morning Father Pomije kept the double doors and one of the side doors locked, and he stood by the side door when the service was over. It took ten minutes to get out of church, but that's the way he wanted it, so he could see who was at Mass that day. He was a brilliant man, educated in Rome, but people wondered about him sometimes. They would say, 'Why doesn't he open those doors?' But my mother defended him, no matter what, always saying, 'He *means* well.'"

As in most communities, there were sharp lines of demarcation drawn between the Catholic and the several Protestant churches in the area, at least on Sunday. But friends were friends and neighbors were neighbors, and the Rauenhorst kids were taught that friends and neighbors look out for each other, regardless of background or religion. One of young Gerry's best friends was a boy whose family had fallen on even harder times than the Rauenhorsts during the Depression. They had very little to call their own, not even a car, and then, one day when the boys were in high school, the boy's father died.

"I went to my folks and asked to borrow the car so I could drive my friend and his family to the funeral," Gerry says. "They were Methodists, and when we got to their church, my friend asked me to come in and sit down with them. Well, today we don't think anything of going into other people's churches, but in those days, in a small town, a lot of people would not do it. They thought it was wrong, almost a sin. But my folks were pretty lenient about things like that, and I myself thought, 'Well, if this is bad, I'm sorry, but my friend needs help.' So I went in with his family and sat down."

The Rauenhorsts' faith did not restrict itself to lip service and empty piety; it manifested itself in action, be it helping the poor or looking out for a troubled pal. Sharing one's bounty was simply expected of you in those days—even when there wasn't much bounty to share. In that regard, Henry Rauenhorst set an example that would inspire and motivate his family for at least two generations.

"My mother told me about the time," Gerry explains, "that Father Pomije came out to the farm and talked my dad into pledging $2,000 for the new church the parish was building. My father was struggling to keep his family afloat, and yet he was asked for—and he provided—what was, at that time and in those circumstances, a staggering amount of money. Well, I've never forgotten that story, knowing what a sacrifice that had to have been for him. Who knows how long it took him to make good on that pledge, though I have no doubt that he did."

Gerry remembers, moreover, his mother's quiet but consistent charity. "She always had soup for any hobos who passed by, so long as they chopped some wood first," he says. "The feeling was that everyone was welcome to what we had, but that everyone should contribute in some way, too."

Hanky's family, farming in nearby Bird Island, operated on similar principles of a living, giving faith. And, not surprisingly, their parents' examples suggested the course that Hanky and Gerry would follow throughout their lifetime.

As young people leaving the farm for the larger, more complicated world of the big city, both Gerry and Hanky could have strayed from their parents' faith, but neither did. In fact, Gerry's faith and principles were strengthened, first, at St. Thomas and, then, at Marquette, institutions that combined rigorous scholarship and a positive social life with an unequivocal moral ethic. Hanky found the same qualities at St. Catherine's. In an obvious way, their college educations were extensions of their parents' teaching and example at home—which, of course, was no accident. "Mother was always insistent on us going to a Catholic university," Gerry points out. And, in addition to bolstering their faith, their higher education would create the connections that would influence their substantial philanthropic efforts in the years to come.

To this day, Gerry and Hanky won't miss Mass on Sunday. "A lot of people—a lot of Catholics—don't think that's a big deal anymore," Gerry has observed. "But that's the way we were taught. It's like telling the truth and playing fair and paying your bills. You go to Mass every week. It's one of the habits—one of the *good* habits—formed during your childhood." After moving to their current home in 1975, Gerry and Hanky became faithful members of Our Lady of Grace Catholic Church in Edina. "It has a homeyness and community to it," Gerry once told The *Catholic Bulletin*. "I feel comfortable knowing people whose church and religion are first and foremost, but who don't avoid the real world, either."

Never lost on Gerry is the knowledge that deeds speak louder than words—and that faith is nothing more than words if it isn't translated into action. To understand Gerry, his family, and the company he and his family have built is to understand that Gerry's faith is the foundation on which his operating philosophy, judgments, relationships, reputation, business, and philanthropy—in other words, the multiple components of his very being—are based.

Word and Deed

Gerry has never drawn a line between the standards of private and public behavior, or created lawyerly distinctions between the ethics of one's personal life and those of the business world.

If you're an honest, upright man or woman in one context, he's always believed, you should be expected to be the same in every other context as well. It was, after all, the disconnect between the moral teachings he followed as an individual and the questionable practices he was exposed to in his first two jobs after college that set him off on his own, seeking that better way.

"Gerry, it's safe to say, has never been a person who sees much of the world in shades of gray," says son Mark with a smile. "He's always been a black-and-white sort of guy."

"Gerry's the kind of guy who wouldn't even cheat in a game of golf," notes Ned Bechtold, owner and chief executive officer of Payne and Dolan, a construction company based in Waukesha, Wisconsin, and a close friend of the Rauenhorst family for many years. "I know, because I've played golf with him a number of times. In every setting, he's a man of absolute integrity, and I've always been led to believe that that's the way he was brought up, the way he's always been. I can see how that integrity has been a part of his business. He's never cut corners in business, and he's never tolerated anyone working for him who does."

"He's a man of character," Richard Schulze, founder and chairman of Best Buy Corporation, a member of St. Thomas's board of trustees, and another one of Gerry's close associates, adds. "He's always been a man beyond reproach. Ethically, he's as sound a businessman as I've ever met. When he says he's going to do something, you can take it to the bank. He's a man without any hidden agenda. What you see is what you get. That's how he thinks and that's how he acts. He's one hundred percent consistent."

Gerry himself has made the point about consistency in behavior again and again over the years, often in public and professional forums, and occasionally in the media as well. Frequently asked to speak about his rags-to-riches experience and the lessons learned in the process of building a successful business, he will often focus on issues of morals and principles—and the need to act on them.

Here is part of the commencement address he delivered at St. Thomas in 1973:

John Dean [former lawyer to President Richard Nixon] opened his testimony before the Senate subcommittee [investigating the

Watergate burglary and cover-up] with the statement, "My daddy told me that the best thing to do when you get cornered is to tell the truth." My theme today will be, "Tell the truth and you will never get cornered."

As you proceed through life, you will be faced, many times, with the fact that the realities of the world are in conflict with your personal ideals. However, human activity must proceed. We cannot wait for perfection—social, political, and environmental problems must be solved, and you must be part of the team that brings all people, with all their imperfections, together into productive units: business, professional, and governmental.

Improvement is needed, but we cannot ignore the need to feed, clothe, and house the growing millions of people in the world today, while we try to reform it. We must provide the essentials of life, even as we try to improve its quality. All of us are concerned with the world we live in. Much of this springs from fear—fear that your personal ideals may be in conflict with the realities of that world. May I urge you to put your fears and concerns aside because the world needs your ideas and ideals now more than ever.

As a businessman and a Christian, I want to say to you that you can be successful in this life and at the same time adhere to the highest professional standards and the highest moral virtue. You don't have to be crooked in order to succeed. You don't have to compromise truth and honesty. Beyond that, it is my considered opinion that you are more apt to succeed if you practice one hundred percent honesty.

As you continue through life, you will have many occasions to see someone else compromise his honesty or morality to achieve an immediate gain. It is possible that the time may come when you could lose your job by being one hundred percent honest. Indeed, many of my competitors have taken jobs away from me by compromising their honesty. Although their gain was immediate, in many cases it was temporary. Several of them are bankrupt today. The reason may be that they eventually compromised themselves to the point of being ineffective. It often hurts to observe a competitor who is willing to cheat a little and pass you by. Life, however, is a long journey. It is my firm conviction that honesty may cause temporary setbacks, but in the long run it is the only way to go.

I stand before you as one firmly committed to honesty and am, I hope, somewhat successful.

In a 1978 speech entitled "The Good Shepherd," he touched on a similar theme:

The idealism we have developed as Christians may seem incompatible with the outside world. You and I, on occasion, have seen many who have gone before us compromise their ideals. How can we be sure we will succeed where others have failed? Only you can answer this question. Let me remind you, however, that the majority of people have not compromised their ideals....

True success and goodness in life do not depend on power and the use of it, but on other factors that spring from the type of people we are. A certain outlook on life, a certain balance of good and evil, and a certain adherence to principle rather than expediency are part of the philosophy of a true Christian....

Twenty-five years ago I started my own business with a great deal of apprehension. One of my great fears was that someday I would be faced with the necessity of compromising my principles in order to survive in business. May I say to you that I have never been required to make that decision. If I had, I know what that decision would have been.

And, in remarks to the Edina Women's Club in 1981, he said:

I'm reminded of Mark Twain's observation that an ethical man is a Christian holding four aces.

Many modern-day cynics are still arguing that ethics have no place in business, that an ethical businessman can be described in terms similar to those used by Mark Twain.

I am here to tell you today that ethics *do* belong in business, and, in fact, it is the introduction of an ethical standard to the business world that elevates the art and practice of business to a profession. Those who operate in the business arena without an ethical standard are simply practicing a vocation. They don't deserve the label "professional."

It was Pope Pius XI in the early part of [the twentieth] century who commented on the fact that…"though it is true that economic science and morality are each guided by its own principles in its own sphere, it is false that the two orders are so distinct and alien that the former, in no way, depends upon the latter.…"

Our late Pope understood that business is simply one institution in a highly interrelated social complex. What is needed is perspective so that the importance of what one is doing in business does not obscure the importance of society as a whole. Appreciation of this fact is necessary for understanding the notions of social responsibility and obligation, two very important ethical concepts. What must be avoided is the narrow view that allows people to think that business is a world unto itself with its own set of rules and values, and the rest of ethics is something for the clergy to watch over.

What are ethics? Simply stated, ethics are the discipline of dealing with what is good or bad, and with moral duty and obligations—in short, a set of moral principles or values. It isn't hard to see that a businessman who accepts a set of moral principles or values to guide the conduct of his business would be creating, or perhaps more accurately, accepting a professional standard of conduct.…

I don't think it's possible to talk about ethics without bring-ing in the concept of morality, and when you talk about morality you have to include the concept of religion. Morality without

The Rauenhorst family crest comprises, beneath the core value integrity, *six elements:*
a tree with two trunks, symbolizing Gerald and Henrietta;
seven branches, representing their seven children;
a dove with an olive branch, symbolizing family peace and tranquility;
the ionic capital, from classic Greek architecture,
representing the Opus Group of Companies;
a hand holding a heart, representing family values of hard work and a love of God;
and a traditional Christian cross, which connects the four symbols within the shield,
resulting in strength and unity in both the family and the business.

Six-month-old Gerry *waits patiently for his dishpan bath.*

Bob, left, and Gerry *on the shoulders of older brother George.*

1935

Gerry, left, and Bob, with a gunnysack
and a pail of water, on "our way to
drown out gophers."

1939

The Henry Rauenhorst family comprised, left to right: William Cletus
(Clete), George, Henry (Hank), Henry Theodore (Gerry's father), Muriel,
Margaret (Gerry's mother), James (Jim), Gerald (Gerry), and Robert (Bob).
Jerome, another one of Gerry's older brothers, was in the Army. The photo
was taken in the Rauenhorst home in Olivia, Minnesota, on the third
tenant farm occupied by the Rauenhorst family during the Great Depression.

1940

The Rauenhorst boys *raised turkeys for a time on the family farm. Though only a high-school freshman at the time, Gerry was put in charge of the operation.*

1943

As kids on the farm, Gerry and Bob, left, were inseparable and often thought to be twins. Bob was a year younger—but always taller—than Gerry.

1949

During Gerry and Hanky's long-distance courtship, Gerry flew his newly purchased $500 airplane back and forth between Milwaukee (where he was studying engineering at Marquette University), Olivia (his hometown), Bird Island (Hanky's

home), and Holman Field in St. Paul (Hanky was working in the Twin Cities after graduating from the College of St. Catherine). Gerry also used the little plane to help pay his tuition, teaching fellow students how to fly.

1950

Honeymoon-bound, Hanky and Gerry get ready to depart for the Canadian Rockies after their wedding celebration in Bird Island, the bride's hometown.

1953

Zion Lutheran Church *in his hometown of Olivia was Gerry's first construction project as an independent entrepreneur. He was twenty-five years old, determined to find a better way to build and run a company, and he and Hanky had invested their $354 savings to launch the business.*

1955

Rauenhorst Construction Company's *second headquarters at 7848 Fremont Avenue South in Bloomington, Minnesota. It was built two years after the company's founding and succeeded Gerry's original HQ—an eight-by-sixteen-foot breezeway in the family home at 6427 18th Avenue South, in the Minneapolis suburb of Richfield. Half of the Fremont Avenue building was leased to Keegan Equipment Company, marking the beginning of Rauenhorst's leasing business.*

1958

Signing a contract for the construction of Dowling Hall on the University of St. Thomas campus in St. Paul, Minnesota, are Gerry and Dr. James Shannon, St. Thomas's president. Dowling, which 340 students would eventually call home, was the first major project for the five-year-old Rauenhorst Construction Company.

1959

To accommodate a rapidly growing company, Rauenhorst Construction built its third headquarters at 5000 West 78th Street in Bloomington.

1961

Gerry's fish-eye camera captured the dimensions of a building constructed for Control Data Corporation, the first structure in what was to become Normandale Industrial Park, a Rauenhorst development, in Bloomington. At the time, it seemed like a remote location, but Gerry believed the Twin Cities'

southwest suburbs were on the brink of rapid growth. And, less than ten years after this photo was snapped, Normandale Industrial Park had become a bustling commercial center comprising more than 400 businesses in fifty-one buildings, all of them built by Rauenhorst Construction.

1962

Robert F. Kennedy, then U.S. Attorney General, visits with Gerry at a gathering of national business leaders in Washington, D.C. The purpose of the meeting— to which Gerry was invited by then Minnesota Senator Hubert H. Humphrey—was to discuss the formation of a domestic Peace Corps and its potential impact on U.S. business.

1963

The first Howard Johnson motor hotel built west of the Mississippi River—in Bloomington, Minnesota—was an important early project

for Rauenhorst Construction. It preceded a second HoJo facility that Rauenhorst built in St. Paul several years later. Both were owned and operated by the builder. In all, Rauenhorst built five HoJos in the sixties.

1964

During a visit to Christ Church College, at England's Oxford University, in 1964, Gerry first envisioned how a university campus in the

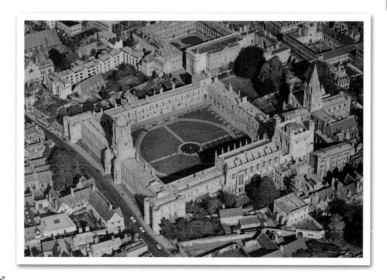

heart of a major urban area might look. That vision became the design concept for the University of St. Thomas campus in downtown Minneapolis.

1965

During groundbreaking ceremonies for the Rauenhorst-built Hazelden Foundation facilities in Center City, Minnesota, Gerry chats with Patrick Butler, Hazelden's longtime president. Gerry's association with the nationally acclaimed treatment center for chemically dependent persons led to his company's creation of Progress Valley.

1966

The familiar hexagonal logo, created in 1966 and viewed here through Gerry's fish-eye camera lens, has been the company's symbol—with some modifications—to this day. For many years the company had an easy-to-remember telephone number: WA7-7777.

1968

Archbishop Harold Henry _with Hanky and Gerry at the dedication in Korea of St. Gerald Church, named after their son, Gerald Anthony Rauenhorst, Jr. who died in 1966 at the age of six weeks. Hanky and Gerry are dressed in traditional Korean robes of honor. Gerry is wearing a hat made of horsehair, a symbol of honor given to Korean men at the age of sixty. Gerry was forty-one at the time._

1968

A helicopter _in front of Rauenhorst's fourth headquarters, which was built in 1963 at 4444 Rauenhorst Circle in Bloomington. The chopper waits for Gerry and William Ylvisaker, chief executive officer of Gould Battery Company, who will view the site that ultimately becomes Gould's headquarters in nearby St. Paul._

1969

The Reverend John P. Raynor, S.J., left, then president of Marquette University, relaxes with Gerry and the Reverend Edward J. O'Donnell, S.J., chancellor and former Marquette president. Gerry, an alumnus, served as a trustee of the Milwaukee institution for thirty years. He was the longest-serving trustee in the history of both Marquette and his other alma mater, the University of St. Thomas.

(Photo courtesy of Marquette University archives.)

1972

The company built Northwestern Financial Center, *at 7900 Xerxes Avenue South in Bloomington, in 1972. It was the tallest building in the Twin Cities suburbs in 1974, the year Gerry moved Rauenhorst Corporation headquarters into its twenty-second and twenty-third floors. The NFC was the company's fifth headquarters site in its first twenty-one years.*

108

1972

A meeting of Rauenhorst Corporation officers, *several of whom also constituted the group that founded Progress Valley, a not-for-profit organization that provides a residence, continued care, and motivation*

to recovering chemically dependent persons after primary treatment. Left to right: George Connor, general counsel; William Schmalberger, chief financial officer; Jim O'Neill, president of development; Gerry, chief executive officer; Nick Simons, president of construction operations; and George Hebert, president of residential operations.

1972

At the company's first annual picnic, *Gerry presents service awards to six long-serving employees. The picnic and awards became an Opus tradition. From the beginning, Gerry's human resources philosophy has been*

simple: Hire good people, pay them fairly, and give them responsibility and authority in equal measure.

1973

Under construction, *at a government-sponsored elderly housing project, is one of the early structures built with products of Fabcon, an Opus subsidiary founded in 1971 to manufacture hollow-core concrete panels for walls, floors, and ceilings.*

1976

Patrick Lucey, who was then governor of Wisconsin, *rode in Gerry's electric car while viewing the unique dual roadway system at the Opus 2 development in Minnetonka.*

Gerry and his family *following the funeral of Gerry's brother Bob, who was killed in a plane crash. Standing, left to right: Judy, Gerry, Hanky, and Joe. Seated, left to right: Amy, Michael, Karen*

Dolan Rauenhorst (Mark's wife), Mark, Susan, and Neil. Karen holds three-week-old Jeff, Hanky and Gerry's first grandchild.

Police and firemen removed bodies from the wreckage of a plane which crashed, killing six top officials of the Olivia, Minn., seed company.

On July 13, 1978, the Minneapolis Tribune *reported the fatal plane crash, near Kenyon, Minnesota, that killed Gerry's brother Bob, (second from the right) two nephews, and three other managers from the Trojan Seed Company of Olivia. Bob, who was forty-nine, was Trojan's chairman; he was credited in the article with building the small family firm into the fifth largest seed company in the world.*

1981

Gerry and Hanky at Marquette University with Mother Teresa, *when the world-famous humanitarian received one of only three Founder's Medals ever awarded by Marquette.*

1982

Opus Center, *the sixth headquarters of what was then called Opus Corporation, was built at 9900 Bren Road East in Minnetonka, another Twin Cities suburb. Opus 2 is a mixed-use community of office, light industrial, and residential areas.*

1982

The company changes its name from Rauenhorst Corporation to Opus—Latin for "a creative work." Founded as Trojan Construction in 1953, the company soon became Rauenhorst Construction, then, in 1965, Rauenhorst Corporation.

1983

Hanky is a fisher-woman, too. Here she proves it, with a 172-pound halibut she caught while on a deep-sea fishing outing off the Alaska coast. Previously, her largest catch was husband Gerry, at 165 pounds.

1983

Mr. Durenberger, Mr. President, recent reports have indicated an alarming deterioration in the quality of education in American schools. These analyses have made us all painfully aware of the critical need to reassess our education policy and search for ways in which we can restore excellence in education.

I strongly believe that the problem with the quality of education and the solution to that problem lie in one simple word, "Choice." The lack of choice has caused the failure in our educational system. Providing choice to every American will restore educational greatness.

Gerald Rauenhorst, chairman of the Opus Corp. in Minneapolis, has served as a member of the Governor's Commission for Evaluation of Elementary and Secondary Teaching and is a member of the Minnesota Business Partnership studying Minnesota's educational system. Mr. Rauenhorst recently wrote an editorial for the Catholics Today magazine which clearly identifies the need for choice in education.

I would like to share his article with my colleagues, and I ask that the text of the article, "Deregulation of Public Schools Might Improve Education," be printed in the RECORD.

The article follows:

Deregulation of Public Schools Might Improve Education

(By Gerald Rauenhorst)

(Rauenhorst, a regular contributor to the Catholic Bulletin, *is chairman of Opus Corporation, a past member of the Governor's Commission for Evaluation of Elementary and Secondary Teaching and a member of the Minnesota Business Partnership studying Minnesota's K-12 educational system.)*

There is one public service provided to U.S. citizens in which the recipient has no choice of provider. A citizen who receives Medicare has the right to select his hospital and doctor. A food stamp recipient may select his own grocery store. Welfare payments and unemployment benefits are provided in dollars; the recipient chooses where to spend them. In one most important service, however, there is no choice whatsoever—education.

Each community has only one public school system. A family living on "A" Avenue and "B" Street is usually required to send its children to "C" school where each child is assigned to teacher "E" or "F." This assignment to school and teacher is regardless of the quality of education provided. The recipient's options are limited to accepting the assignment or to abandoning the system and forfeiting the government's support of this service. A family may choose a private school alternative—as long as the private school is government approved—and pay directly for education. However, for many the financial burden is so heavy that the private school is not a viable alternative.

The education system in America today has been soundly criticized by the National Commission on Excellence in Education, which wrote "if an unfriendly foreign power had attempted to impose on America the mediocre educational performance that exists today, we might well have viewed it as an act of war. As it stands, we have allowed this to happen to ourselves." Given the composition of this commission—prominent educators and public spirited citizens—this is indeed a serious indictment of American public education.

I suggest that the time is right for deregulation of education. In this age of concern for the consumer, our government has seen fit to deregulate the telephone company and the airlines, and is working on the banks. AT&T has been cut up into eight separate companies, even though, unlike our public education system, no one disputes the fact that it is the world's best telephone company. With deregulation, the airlines are now free to fly to any city they choose. The consumer has responded with delight to the options which have resulted from competition; he can choose to fly to Florida for $99 or $300.

It's my contention that until such time as the educational system is deregulated and the consumer is allowed an element of choice in schools and in teachers, we will see little, if any, improvement. A voucher system would be one way to introduce consumer choice in the selection of education services. However, given the strong opposition to a voucher system and the lobbying strength of the Minnesota Educational Association (MEA) locally and the National Education Association nationally, the voucher alternative has little chance of passing.

In Minnesota, after years of concerted effort to populate the legislature with teachers and former educators, the MEA has amassed considerable political power. As near as I can tell, there are more than 40 Minnesota legislators with public education ties. Somehow we must utilize or neutralize that power and find ways to move—however slowly—toward increasing each family's options, when selecting schools. Gradually, we must provide real freedom of choice. Only then we will significantly improve education quality for all.

Four years ago, I served on the governor's commission to evaluate elementary and secondary teaching in Minnesota. I was appalled to learn that there is only one criterion for the retention of teachers—seniority. In a layoff situation, a school's worst teacher who has been there 12 years would be retained while a school's best teacher with lesser seniority, say 11 years, would be terminated.

If indeed the situation is as bad as the national commission states, and I believe it is, it's time for every citizen to take an active part in correcting the system. I suggest that we begin by promoting competition, rewarding superior performance, and eliminating seniority as the sole criterion for teacher retention.

Unless these weaknesses are corrected by action of the citizens of this nation who are paying for our educational systems, we can expect the education of our youth to continue to deteriorate.

The Congressional Record published Gerry's outspoken advocacy of deregulation of education across America. Above is an excerpt.

1987

Gerry caught this tarpon—*which weighed more than he did—during a fishing contest in Florida. The catch netted him a $20,000 prize, which was shared with the captain and six other members of the fishing party.*

1989

Breakfast at the Vatican *with Pope John Paul II was a highlight of Gerry's life. On the left in this photo is John Cardinal O'Connor, the Pope, and Archbishop (now Cardinal) Theodore McCarrick. Across the table, in the red hat, is Cardinal John Krol. Gerry is seated beneath the window at the far end of the table.*

1990

A landmark development on thirty-five acres in downtown Omaha, Nebraska, the ConAgra campus was designed and built by Opus Corporation. The project, which revitalized the city's derelict core, opened on September 17, 1990. It was

designed by John Albers, Opus president of architecture and engineering, in close collaboration with ConAgra's CEO at the time, Mike Harper, who wanted the development to reflect Nebraska's prairie landscape. Appropriately enough, the project's distinctive architecture was inspired by Frank Lloyd Wright's Prairie School style.

1991

Pope John Paul II with Hanky and Gerry in the Parish House at St. Patrick's Cathedral during a papal visit to New York City.

1992

Opus *received the National Developer of the Year award from the National Association of Industrial and Office Properties.*

1993

The growing Opus family *celebrates forty years in business at Opus headquarters. As the organization has expanded, it has emphasized teamwork and respect for individuals. Many employees have worked at Opus for decades.*

1994

J.W. Marriott, Jr., chairman and president of Marriott International, Inc., with Gerry *at the cornerstone celebration of Opus-built Maplewood Park Place, an innovative housing development for seniors in Bethesda, Maryland. The 210-unit project was completed in 1995.*

1995

The Rauenhorst children *(right) gather before a fresco portrait of the young family painted on one of the pillars in Terrence Murphy Hall on the University of St. Thomas's Minneapolis campus. The background fresco portrait was commissioned by St. Thomas to honor the Rauenhorst family for its generosity. Standing, left to right: Joe, Mark, Neil, and Michael. Seated, left to right: Susan, Judy, and Amy.*

119

TOP DEVELOPER SURVEY

NATIONAL REAL ESTATE INVESTOR is pleased to present its eighth annual Top Developer Survey, ranking the most active developers in 1995. Due to space, only the top 25 firms are listed here, but copies of the entire survey can be purchased from Argus Direct Marketing Department at (770) 618-0381.

OPUS GROUP OF COS.

1

9900 Bren Rd. E., Minnetonka, MN 55343
612 936-4444; Fax: 612 936-4529
Regs./Branches: Opus North Corp.: Chicago, Columbus, Milwaukee; Opus Northwest, L.L.C.: Seattle, Denver, Minneapolis; Opus South Corp.: Tampa, Pensacola, Orlando, Ft. Lauderdale, Dallas, Atlanta; Opus Southwest Corp.: Phoenix, San Francisco, Sacramento; Opus East, L.L.C., Washington, D.C.
Contacts: Gerald Rauenhorst, CEO/Opus Corp.; Keith Bednarowski, Pres. & CEO/Opus U.S. Corp.; Mark Rauenhorst, Pres. & COO/Opus Corp.; Tom Roberts, Pres. & COO/Opus Southwest Corp.; Neil Rauenhorst, Pres. & COO/Opus South Corp.; Jim Nygaard, CEO/Opus North Corp.; Joe Rauenhorst, Pres. & COO/Opus East, L.L.C.; Gene Haugland, Pres. & CEO/Opus Nat'l L.L.C.
Total Sq. Ft. under Constr. '94: 8,329,763
Constr. Starts '94: 5,749,017
Constr. Starts '95: 7,957,192
Type of Projects:
  O - 14%
  I - 50%
  R - 36%
Major Projects '94: Carol Point Dist. Ctr., Carol Stream, IL

Highland Grove, Highland, IN
General Motors Warehouse, El Paso, TX
Attorney General State of California, Sacramento, CA
Arcadia Crossing, Phoenix, AZ

HINES INTERESTS LTD. PARTNERSHIP

2

2800 Post Oak Blvd., Houston, TX 77056-611
713 621-8000; Fax: 713 966-2053
Regs./Branches: Atlanta, Chicago, New York Francisco, Berlin, Paris and Moscow
Contacts: Gerald D. Hines, Chmn.; Jeffrey C Hines, Pres.; EVPs: Kenneth W. Hubbar S. Sklar; C. Kevin Shannahan; E. Stama Ogilvie; James C. Buie; Michael J.G. T C. Hastings Johnson, CFO; SVPs: Day Leasing; John A. Harris, Design & C Ann McGonigle Kifer, VP/Mktg. & Comm.
Total Sq. Ft. under Constr. '94: 8,106,3
Constr. Starts '94: 3,536,000
Constr. Starts '95: 4,796,000
Type of Projects:
  O - 62%
  R - 15%
  M - 8%
  University Facilities - 4%
  Mixed Use - 11%
Major Projects '94: Hofgarten am Gendarmenmarkt, Berlin, Germ Owens-Corning World Hqtrs., T First Colony Mall, Houston, TX San Francisco Civic Ctr., San F Allen-Bradley Reg. Hqtrs., Cle

ALPHABETICAL LIST OF 1995 TOP DEVELOPERS WITH RANKINGS

CBL & Assoc. Properties, Inc.   10

INDUSTRIAL DEVEI INT'L (IDI)

3343 Peachtree Rd. N.E., St 30326
404 233-6080; Fax: 404 23

Opus was named the nation's number one developer *by* National Real Estate Investor *magazine.*

1995

Alan Greenspan, chairman of the U.S. Federal Reserve Board, at Gerry's *retirement as chairman of the Ninth Federal Reserve District. Gerry served on the Ninth District board from 1990 to 1995.*

1996

Warren Buffett, chairman of Berkshire Hathaway Inc., jokes with Gerry *at a charity golf tournament in Omaha. They are holding Buffett's wallet. On a later occasion, the legendary investment guru auctioned off the same wallet, with a stock tip inside, for $250,000.*

1998

Gerry displays the ten-pound walleye he caught while vacationing with Hanky at their northern Minnesota lake home, Marienwald. (The name is German for St. Mary's Woods and honors the Rauenhorst ancestral home in Germany.)

1998

The company's seventh headquarters, at 10350 Bren Road West, in the Opus 2 development of Minnetonka. After fifteen years in multi-tenant buildings, Opus moved back to a home of its own, which its founder believes is a better fit for the Opus culture.

1998

Pope John Paul II's kindness—and sense of humor—*were apparent during one of the Rauenhorsts' several trips to Rome. En route to Mass at St. Peter's, Hanky fell and cut her nose. "I put a little piece of Kleenex on the cut and went in," she said. Afterward, when informed what had happened, the Pope promptly bestowed a blessing on Hanky's injured nose.*

1999

Nicholas, son of Amy and Philip Goldman, *receives his first navigational training from "Bumpa" on Gerry's boat in Florida.*

1999

Gerry in an unguarded moment *during a Canadian fishing trip with his sons. His longtime administrative assistant, Judy Truex, dubbed the photo "Rauenhorst on a Rock," noting that it gives "rest and relaxation a whole new meaning."*

1999

With George H.W. Bush, *the forty-first President of the United States, are Gerry, Hanky, and Dr. Rolland Dickson of the Mayo Clinic at a gathering in Kennebunkport, Maine. Gerry serves on the Mayo*

Foundation Advisory Council to the President of the renowned clinic, which is chaired by former First Lady Barbara Bush.

2000

The entire Gerald Rauenhorst family *celebrates Hanky and Gerry's fiftieth wedding anniversary on a barge,* The Lorraine, *in France.*

2000

Gerry confers with his oldest son, Mark, *as the latter took the position of president and chief executive officer of Opus Corporation. Gerry assumed the title of founding chairman.*

Still very much in love: *Hanky and Gerry at their fiftieth wedding celebration.*

**Hanky entertains
friends on Gerry's
boat**—*which he
named in her
honor—at their
Florida home.*

Exchanging a hug *at the wedding of Susan Rauenhorst Turner are Gerry
and Muriel Baumgartner, his only surviving sibling.*

2001

During commencement ceremonies at Marquette University, the Reverend Robert A. Wild, S.J., left, the school's president, confers an honorary doctor of laws degree on Gerry, who earned an engineering degree there in 1951. With them is John J. Stollenwerk, CEO of Allen Edmunds Corporation and a member of the Marquette board of trustees.

(Photo courtesy of Marquette University archives.)

2002

Gerry with scholar and author Michael Novak, left, and William F. Buckley, author, pundit, and founder of the National Review, at a Becket Fund for Religious Liberty dinner in New York City.

Monsignor Terrence Murphy, *former president and then chancellor of the University of St. Thomas and a longtime friend of the Rauenhorst family, says Mass at Marienwald, Hanky and Gerry's Minnesota lake home.*

The Reverend Dennis Dease, *left, president of the University of St. Thomas, with Gerry and Dr. Christopher Puto, dean of UST's College of Business, signing the document that funded the Opus Distinguished Chair for the Dean of the College of Business.*

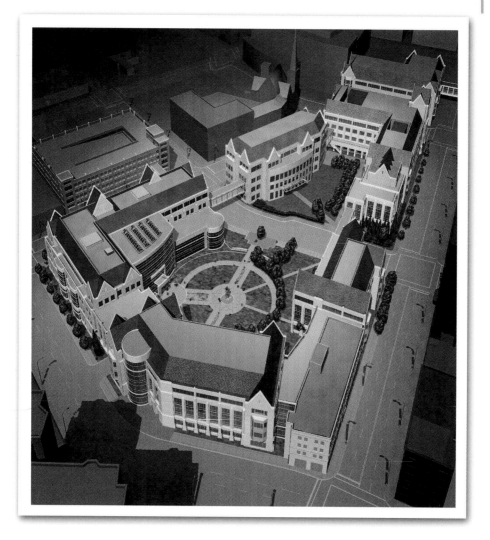

An artist's conception *of the finished University of St. Thomas campus in downtown Minneapolis being built by Opus. In the upper left, adjacent to a city-operated parking ramp that Opus built, is the St. Thomas School of Law, completed in 2003; to its right, a design concept of the future School of Entrepreneurship; at the top, Opus Hall, completed in 1999, housing the School of Education; south of Opus Hall is Terrence Murphy Hall, completed in 1992, which houses the graduate programs of the College of Business and the Graduate School of Professional Psychology; at the lower right and lower center, design concepts of possible future St. Thomas buildings.*

The 3.6-million-square-foot campus of Best Buy Corporation, *the nation's largest consumer electronics company, in the south Minneapolis suburb of Richfield, was designed and built by Opus. The complex brought fourteen disparate suburban locations into one comprehensive urban setting.*

An aerial view of Phase I of the Northwestern Mutual Corporation campus under construction by Opus in suburban Milwaukee. Announced in the summer of 2002, the project will consist of four phases and comprise eight structures, including four office buildings and four parking facilities.

2003

Hanky and Gerry with Sister Andrea Lee, *president of the College of St. Catherine, with a drawing of the new Opus-built Student Center on the school's St. Paul campus. Hanky was a*

1949 graduate of St. Catherine and is a trustee emerita of the college.

2003

Luz Campa, *Opus senior vice president for tax, right, and company chairman Keith Bednarowski discuss issues related to the Rauenhorst family trusts. The family's second generation has designated Campa and Bednarowski— who are longtime*

friends as well as veteran Opus officials—trustees of the two family trusts.

religion is a tree without roots, a stream without a spring to feed it, or a house built on the sand. It was Montesquieu who said, "The morality of the Gospel is the noblest gift ever bestowed by God on man." The Bible certainly is the proper place to start when developing a standard of conduct for business.

The religions of our rich Judeo-Christian culture give us the time-honored principles of right and wrong in the conduct of our everyday affairs. They certainly are the source of an ethical standard to be followed in American business today.... Enthusiasm, hard work, and enterprise are not enough. You have got to have a sense of direction. It's that ethical standard that gives us a sense of direction....

There was never any doubt about the ethical standards in place in the Rauenhorst organization. One small but telling example Gerry likes to recall is his hiring and lengthy employment of Martha Durocher, his first receptionist-secretary (after Hanky). Martha had been divorced, and Gerry, like a lot of good Catholics at the time, was concerned about the propriety of adding a divorced person to the (then small) corporate family. He dutifully consulted with his pastor, who assured him that there would be no problem from the church's point of view as long as the individual didn't remarry. Relieved, Gerry promptly hired Durocher, and she quickly became a valued member of the team.

Then, three or four years later, at the company's Christmas party, Durocher introduced Gerry to a male friend named Duke, to whom she was obviously very close. Gerry said to himself, "Good God, Martha got married. What am I going to do now?" The next day Martha asked him what he thought of the man she'd brought to the party. Before he could respond, she added, "Duke, you know, was my former husband. I remarried him, thanks in large part to what I've learned at this company."

Later, Gerry said, "Times have changed. The Catholic church has relaxed its rules, so I wouldn't have the same problem today. But, believe me, I was very proud to know that our corporate culture had such a positive influence on our people."

The Road to Progress Valley

In 1978, the *Catholic Bulletin* featured Gerry in its "Profiles in Faith" series. Of Gerry and his company, Peter N. Paula wrote:

The melodic jingle of the cash register has kept the Rauenhorst empire growing healthily these many years, but it's certainly not the only, or even the most important, tune to which Gerald Rauenhorst moves. His drummer is deep inside, and the sounds he marches to have more to do with ethics than they have to do with money. He is a businessman with a conscience who is committed to sharing his success with his fellow men.

"We have both a corporate responsibility and a social responsibility to our community," he said.

With Rauenhorst, this is no mere high-sounding ideal. He backs it up with money (lots of it) and plenty of his own time.

During his many years in business, Rauenhorst has devoted considerable time and energy to religious, educational, and charitable activities, and in the past few years has turned over increasing responsibility to his co-workers so he can have the time he needs for these outside labors.

Besides his extensive involvement with St. Thomas and Marquette, the *Catholic Bulletin* tribute described his past presidency of the Minneapolis Suburban Serra Club and former governorship of District 7, Serra International, his long membership in the Knights of Columbus, his involvement with Sogang Jesuit College in Korea, and his Papal Knighthood in the Equestrian Order of the Holy Sepulchre.

For him, life has always been a matter of priorities [the *Catholic Bulletin* story continued]. "We put too much emphasis on material goods these days," [he said]. "They just don't make the difference. It's more important that a person be happy with his mate and the people he lives and works with than he have a lot of material things...."

As both a businessman and a Christian, Gerry has spent much of his working life giving his charitable instincts a sense of direction that is appropriate to both his deeply felt personal concerns and the needs of the communities in which his company does business. To that end, he has long subscribed to the notion that some giving is more effective—and more personally satisfying—than others.

"Just writing a check and saying, 'Fine, let's go play golf,' is really not enough for me," he once told a reporter. "There's no personal feeling. It's no way to involve people as well as money in helping people who need help." Foremost among his several operating principles is the familiar Asian proverb that if you give a man a fish, he eats for a day, but if you teach him how to fish, he is able to eat for life.

Recently, Luz Campa, Gerry's longtime friend and tax advisor, noted that many people seem to believe that wealthy individuals make charitable gifts only for the sake of a tax deduction. Campa says, however, that he has often gone to Gerry and said, "You can't make any more charitable gifts this year—you won't get a deduction," and Gerry has replied, "That's tough. But I have obligations and I'm going to make those gifts anyway."

In the early 1980s, Gerry was quoted in *Industry Week* magazine saying: "The old idea of a corporation existing just to make a buck for the shareholders...is over. Corporations must...help out in solving social problems...and give some of their talents and profits to the social responsibilities of the country. It's vital if we are to keep our license to operate as a free enterprise."

About the same time, in an interview with the *St. Paul Pioneer Press*, he described the imperatives of a business owner's charity, which, as he saw it, begins (though certainly doesn't end) within one's own firm. "It's a broadening experience," he said. "Today you have to be much more concerned with the people in your corporation. It's not a sweatshop. You have to do things to keep employees motivated. The real sense of business is being involved.

"We all tend to write a check to the United Way or some college or other charity and say we've done a good thing. Now that is a good thing, but when we built this company from ground zero, we had to also develop some good people. So we tried to do a little of what Mother Teresa does— cure a social problem not with just money, but by getting involved."

By "this company," it's important to note, Gerry was not speaking of Opus. He was talking about Progress Valley, the alcohol-rehabilitation program that he and his executives developed out of an innovative corporate philanthropy initiative called the 1/40 Program. The latter was created at the company (then still called the Rauenhorst Corporation) in 1970.

According to a company account:

> Believing that the business expertise of its people could bring unique solutions to a variety of social problems, Rauenhorst made a commitment to contribute $1 out of every $40 in net earnings to a separately administered non-profit corporation that would then fund a specific project.
>
> The new organization would be administered by Rauenhorst officers who would choose its president and administrative group. In addition, the Rauenhorst Corporation would release its corporate officers for one hour per week to assist with the project. Those officers would, in turn, contribute an hour of their own time.
>
> After a year of research, the group chose to deal with alcohol rehabilitation. It established Progress Valley, Inc., to provide con-tinuing care and motivation to recovering alcoholics after their release from a primary treatment facility.

In introducing the program to Rauenhorst employees, Gerry wrote: "We thought a business-oriented, problem-solving group of people, approaching a problem in which they had never been involved, might develop a better way to solve this problem. We came to the conclusion that there were enough excellent alcohol-treatment centers in Minnesota. But there did seem to be a need to provide a combination working-living situation for those people who had been through treatment."

In seeking professional leadership, Progress Valley, Inc., learned about Don Stuhlman, a talented businessman who was a recovering alcoholic. Stuhlman became executive director of Progress Valley in January 1972 and began looking for a facility. He found a six-unit apartment building in south Minneapolis and a small furniture manufacturing concern in St. Paul—facilities that would provide both a place to live and a place to work for Progress Valley clients during their return to normal lives.

Within two years, Progress Valley had nearly forty graduates and was on its way to self-sufficiency.

"I had been in business for seventeen years and things were going great," Gerry explained later. "Looking around, I saw all of these wonderful and talented people working for me, helping the business to prosper. But not everyone is so lucky. The world is full of problems, and some people are less fortunate through no fault of their own. I felt a deep moral obligation to help in a concrete way so I challenged my management team."

The company had been contributing to community programs virtually from its beginning in 1953. During the sixties and seventies, Gerry became part of a like-minded group of relatively young, entrepreneurial Twin Cities executives whose innovative business practices and consequent success were matched by their interest in grappling with community needs. David Koch, CEO of Graco Company in Minneapolis, and other local executives created the Keystone Club comprising several business leaders who pledged to give five percent of their companies' before-tax profits to charity. Gerry was a charter member of the group, and Rauenhorst Corporation contributed to the maximum five percent of before-tax profits (later increased to ten percent).

The 1/40 Program and Progress Valley were something else again, however—something new both in the community and for Rauenhorst. But if some observers may have doubted either Gerry's foresight or commitment, they didn't know the man very well.

Patrick Butler, who was then the driving force behind the world-renowned Hazelden treatment facility in Center City (for which

Rauenhorst constructed several buildings), later noted that Gerry and his people "knew nothing about addiction, but the objective was clear, and they had the skills and expertise to attack any problem." William Schmalberger, Rauenhorst's senior vice president at the time, was elected president of the new non-profit. Gerry and Hanky as well as corporate officers Nick Simons, George Hebert, Jim O'Neill, Bob Perkins, Marcel Sciez, and George Connor made up its original board.

Predictably perhaps, given the fact that the early seventies was a time when many American companies were getting involved in unprecedented ways with social causes, Rauenhorst's "better way" drew a great deal of attention.

Jane Maddox is the author of a 1999 report prepared by the Phil-anthropic Initiative, Inc., of Boston entitled, "Straight on 1/40: The Road to Progress Valley." Maddox called the program "a unique and tangible approach that one family-owned business...came up with to 'give back' to society...[that] has [turned] around thousands of lives devastated by substance abuse and alcohol addiction." Importantly, it is also an example, she said, of "making a commitment to *own* a philanthropic work, rather than taking a short-term lease, and sticking to it for the long haul."

Her report continued:

> Minnesotans have a tradition of social responsibility. It's part of their fiber, and it extends from individuals to the corporate world. [But] 1/40 is more than tradition, for tradition can be honored or ignored. Instead, it is a serious down-to-the-bone commitment that has gone to work every day for nearly thirty years. Commitment and partnership are the twin engines of its success.
>
> The name is not flashy, but 1/40 is much more than a name. In principle, what it means is one hour out of every forty worked and one dollar out of every forty earned go back to society. In practice, the ratio for both time and dollars is much higher—ten percent of pre-tax dollars in total company giving and more time than anyone can remember. But, whatever the ratio, making the

name a number has made the commitment more quantifiable. Giving is not reserved for when there is extra time or money, but is invested in every week one in forty—feet to the fire.

Like so many of America's great ideas, the 1/40 concept came from the life experiences of a successful entrepreneur. Gerry Rauenhorst grew up one of eight children in a home where charitable giving was expected, even when money was tightest. From the earliest days, his company contributed to the community, but in 1970 he decided to ratchet up both the focus and the intensity of his community involvement.

He wanted to bring an entrepreneurial approach to what is often a passive and reactive activity. He also wanted to involve the company, especially the talent and drive of his executive team. And, lastly, he wanted to find an important social issue where the results could be measured and the impact understood.

He issued a challenge to his executive staff to come back with a business plan for solving an intractable problem in society...and they decided to dedicate their financial and human resources to starting a new and promising program to help people recovering from addiction to make the transition from treatment to sobriety. The result was Progress Valley, which, over these twenty-eight years, has helped more than 5,000 people overcome their addiction and return to a functioning and fulfilling life....

"God, family, and work, in that order, are most important to me," Gerry affirmed recently, during a review of the family's and company's philanthropy.

"I have always felt we have a deep moral obligation to help other people and to give back to the community. Education has been a priority, and we have supported the University of St. Thomas, the College of St. Catherine, and Marquette University, among others. We also fund Catholic Charities [which provides social services directly to those needing them, rather than making grants to other organizations] and other groups." Opus employees are, in fact, active in a wide range of charitable and civic activities, providing both hands-on and financial assistance to organizations ranging from Habitat for Humanity to the United Way. The company not only encourages its employees to get involved, but often supports that involvement with matching grants. "I truly believe that you get back more than you give. The Lord has been good to me."

Regarding the connection between a family business and philanthropy, he said:

> I view the enterprise as a precious heirloom, it means that much to me—as something to pass on to the next generation, if that's possible, but also for what it allows us to do together for the community. We share in this enterprise—it has a heart and soul.
>
> It's not about making three cents more per share. Sure, we want to make money, but that can't be your God. Private enterprise people feel this way. Our employees feel this way, and they want to stick around longer because of our values. We are very successful, but there's no special patent or secret except hard work and good people. Yes, it also helps our bottom line. Decision-makers recognize us as the people who did such and such, but that's not the reason we give. Ninety percent of the people we build for don't know Progress Valley exists.
>
> I've been somewhat reticent about promoting Progress Valley and 1/40 in the past, but now I think it needs to be communicated better. I would like other private companies to see what can be accomplished with this kind of commitment, focus, and talent so they will think about starting something of their own. It would be wonderful if next year there were ten more companies that had their own 1/40 and then in ten years a hundred companies. So much good could be done.

In its first thirty years, he noted, more than 6,000 persons had graduated from Progress Valley programs in the Twin Cities and Phoenix.

"Mr. St. Thomas"

No institution, organization, or cause, however, can display more tangible results of the Rauenhorsts' faith in action than the University of St. Thomas. Gerry and his company have literally completed twenty projects on the school's St. Paul and Owatonna campuses and the entire four-structure complex in downtown Minneapolis. Over and above all that, he and his family have given the institution millions of dollars in gifts, plus uncounted hours of guidance, governance, and encouragement.

Gerry would say, of course, that few men or women have benefited more than he from the lessons learned and the relationships established at his beloved undergraduate alma mater, and suggest that he's received at least as much as he's given.

But, in the words of Father Dennis Dease, the university's current president, Gerry's multiple contributions to UST over the past fifty years can be described as "philanthropy in the oldest and best sense of the word—that is, in the sense of giving back to the community not just with a check but with your heart."

"I remember when I started as president [in July 1991]," Dease continues with a smile. "The two of us had a private lunch together in Florida, and Gerry said, quietly and simply, 'Now don't screw it up.' He said, 'St. Thomas is a wonderful place and there's never been any ill said of it. I know you'll do well, but this is really quite a trust.' I almost felt as though I was a future son-in-law who had just asked for his daughter's hand and he was saying, 'I think you'll do just fine, but mind you take good care of her.'"

He and Gerry, Father Dease adds, have since become close friends, just as Gerry has enjoyed warm relationships with Dease's predecessors, James Shannon and Terrence Murphy, and countless other administrators, fellow trustees, benefactors, and alumni, as well as faculty members and students at UST.

Gerry's association with St. Thomas "now goes back more than fifty-five years, when he enrolled as an undergraduate, and includes thirty-six years of service on our Board of Trustees," Dease wrote in September 2002.

He went on to say:

What is remarkable about his tenure is that he has been intimately involved with virtually every decision that has led to the growth of St. Thomas from a small undergraduate men's college into a comprehensive regional university with 11,366 students in bachelor's, master's, and doctoral programs....

Along with his involvement in every major change that has transformed St. Thomas since the early 1970s, [Gerry] has been extraordinarily generous as a financial supporter of the university. His primary interest has been in business education. The Rauenhorst family endowed the Opus Chair in Family Enterprise in 1995, and the Opus Corporation endowed the Opus Distinguished Chair for the Dean of the College of Business. But his interests have gone beyond business to the need to educate teachers themselves, as evidenced by his support of the Minneapolis Education Center project. In addition, he has been involved in three capital campaigns....

I should note that [Gerry's] involvement also has gone beyond activities related to strategic planning and philanthropy. He has long taken an interest in alumni activities, having served as a past president of our alumni association and being a past recipient (in 1978) of the association's Distinguished Alumnus Award, its highest honor. He has taught and lectured on entrepreneurship in our College of Business, and he has emphasized the need for ethical behavior in any discipline and any endeavor of life....

He has been a model citizen in this community, a kind, caring, and humble man who always puts the interests of others—his family, his friends, his employees, and his fellow alumni—above his own.

Never has he asked for favors, and never has he expected recognition. He deserves the latter.

Quentin Hietpas, senior vice president emeritus at St. Thomas as well as another close friend of Gerry's, recently had this to say about Gerry's contributions to the university:

> As busy as he has been raising a family of seven children with his wife Henrietta and building a corporation that is number one nationally in its field, Gerry very rarely misses a board meeting. He is focused and extremely creative. He quickly analyzes complex issues and is the most results-oriented person I know. He always does his homework. He is always thoroughly prepared.
>
> When asked by a reporter why he would spend so much of his time as a volunteer on university work, Gerry quickly replied that he felt a moral obligation to pay back, to help improve each of these institutions for the education he had received. That sense of dedication to the University of St. Thomas has clearly earned him the respect of his colleagues on its forty-three-person board....
>
> His fellow trustees particularly respect his vision. Several years ago, Gerry challenged the then small, all-men's college to seek growth and greatness. He pointed out that the state of Minnesota at that time had only one large state-supported public institution of higher learning—the University of Minnesota. Unlike most other states, Minnesota did not have a large, strong, private coeducational comprehensive companion university. He challenged the trustees, administration, and faculty to fill that void. People scoffed at the time. Today, however, most observers would agree that this has occurred.
>
> Gerry worked closely with his fellow trustees and with two presidents—first, Monsignor Terrence Murphy for twenty-five years and then Father Dennis Dease for the past twelve years—on scores of important issues. In the process, St. Thomas has grown from a struggling college of 2,300 students to today's strong, comprehensive university with more than 11,000 students on four campuses. The decision to become coeducational was made in

1977, and the decision to launch an MBA program a year later. Gerry's counsel was in the vanguard of both.

Over the past nineteen years, I have watched Gerry work patiently with presidents Murphy and Dease, and those of us on the staff, to help obtain consensus from his colleagues on the board for, one, a second major campus which evolved from a store-front building that he made available to St. Thomas, rent-free, in downtown Minneapolis; two, the School of Law that came into existence in 2001 after he had first advocated it some twenty-five years earlier; three, a Rome campus site which he personally inspected before it came to the board for approval; four, graduate programs in engineering which emerged from a case he made, drawing on his background as an engineer; five, two capital campaigns in which he worked actively to raise a third of a billion dollars; six, a School of Entrepreneurship; and, seven, the architecture found on the Minneapolis campus that evolved after he personally visited Oxford twice to study its architecture....

Hietpas added that Gerry's association with St. Thomas has been so tight over the years he has locally earned the sobriquet "Mr. St. Thomas."

Judge Diana Murphy, of the United States Court of Appeals for the Eighth District, and a UST trustee for eleven years, added this:

[Gerry] has the courage to think outside the box. If he is persuaded that something should be done to serve unmet needs or to improve an offering of the university, his response is to plan how it can be done—not to focus on the obstacles. In 1978 he urged that the university offer a graduate program in business that would be open to working men and women who could only attend in the evening. It turned out this was a very large untapped market, and the program helped many to advance in their careers. It also was a trailblazer in drawing on the experience of successful business people, adding a practical element to this academic program that was later emulated by other institutions. Later he saw a similar need for graduate programs in software engineering and manufacturing systems. And recently he provided key support for St. Thomas to reopen its School of Law, which is committed to developing a program founded in ethical values and service to the less advantaged. Some of the trustees from the business world were reluctant to be involved in creating more lawyers, and they had to be persuaded that law can be a noble profession. Gerry's open mind and his support were both important in those discussions.

St. Thomas was historically an all-male institution, but Gerry saw that times had changed and that for St. Thomas and its students to flourish, enrollment should be opened to women. That decision was taken in 1977 with his key support, and he continues to favor initiatives for diversity and community service. One outstanding example is his involvement in the university's decision to open a second campus in the heart of downtown Minneapolis. This campus serves some entirely different needs than the ones in St. Paul. One of its programs is a cooperative undertaking with a diverse group of school districts to develop a magnet school downtown. Not only did he make available a building for the classes in Minneapolis, but his generosity later made Opus Hall possible. That hall is attached to the magnet school and houses education faculty and classrooms. His company also designed and built the first permanent building for the Minneapolis campus and is now doing the same for the new law school.

"You know he has the university's welfare at heart all the time," says Dick Schulze, founder of Best Buy Corporation, of Gerry's work as a fellow trustee and benefactor. "He's constantly thinking about how to make it a better place. I think that's one reason Gerry and I get along so well. We're both driven to achieve a higher and greater outcome—for our respective companies and for St. Thomas."

Gerry has also been generous with both his time and resources to his *other* alma mater, Marquette University in Milwaukee. There, too, his mark is tangible on campus, the company having designed and constructed ten buildings over the past nearly fifty years.

As at St. Thomas, Gerry has long been a close advisor to the institution's leadership and an unofficial but highly influential "recruiter" of additional executive talent. "I didn't even go to Marquette," remarks his friend Ned Bechtold. "But now, thanks to Gerry, I'm a trustee! When Gerry first mentioned me for the position, I said, 'Gerry, I'm a Lutheran and I didn't go to school there.' He just said, 'That's O.K., I think you'd still be a good trustee.' So now I am."

In 1969, Marquette named Gerry its Alumnus of the Year "in recognition of leadership in alumni activities, professional achievements, community service, and loyalty to the ideals of Marquette University." Then forty-one, Gerry was the youngest honoree in the award's twenty-five-year history.

Breakfast With the Pope

The faith that has inspired such high-profile public benevolence and involvement has never lost its private meaning for Gerry. His relationship with God is first and last a personal one, the same as it's always been, based not on a presumption of entitlement but on a humble deference to the higher power.

"Do you pray regularly?" a friend asked him recently.

"Yes," he replied.

"Have you always prayed?"

"Yes."

"Do you pray about business decisions?"

"No. I don't pray about that."

"You never said, 'God, please help me win this bid?'"

"The most I might have said in that regard is, 'Lord, let me say the right things and do the right things.' I've never prayed to win a bid or anything like that. I pray for my family, and I pray for my friends. And I'm very accepting. I've always been willing to live with what God sends me."

It was that personal faith that helped sustain Gerry and Hanky through the loss of their parents and most of their siblings, including the death of Gerry's brother Hank, who was killed in an automobile accident involving a drunk driver in 1962, and the private airplane crash that took the lives, in July 1978, of Gerry's brother Bob, two nephews, and three other members of their Olivia-based seed business. Shortly after Bob's death, a neighbor told Gerry and Hanky that the tragic loss of his brothers reminded her of the tragedies that had befallen the Kennedy family. Gerry's grief, in each case, was deep and lasting. "I was inconsolable," he said much later.

In the spring of 1966, their faith may have faced its toughest test, when the Rauenhorsts' eighth child, Gerald Anthony Rauenhorst, died six weeks after his birth. The tragic airplane accident and their child's death reaffirmed the sense that while the ways of God are unknowable to humans, every day that we have on earth is God's gift as well. Gerry said recently, "Hanky and I seldom drive past Resurrection Cemetery without stopping to have a chat with our little saint in heaven. I look at the name *Gerald Anthony Rauenhorst* carved in granite on that gravestone, and it's a sobering thought. But it's a good thought, too. He was ours for a little while, and now he is with God."

Meanwhile, the Rauenhorsts' many lay activities on behalf of the Catholic church have taken them around the world, to places as diverse as Seoul and Rome.

In 1968, Hanky described the couple's first trip to Korea, to visit Sogang College in Seoul and Archbishop Henry in Kwangju. In a Catholic newsletter after that trip, Hanky wrote, "My husband and I feel especially fortunate having seen with our own eyes and felt in our hearts the powerful influence that Christianity plays in the lives of these hospitable and hard-working people."

For Gerry, who served as chairman of the American advisory board of the Sogang institution, the Korean experience provided another opportunity to put his faith to practical action. In the late sixties, Sogang was receiving $90,000 a year from Jesuits in the United States. As a better alternative, Gerry suggested that the school, led by Father Del Skillingstad, the institution's chief financial officer (and, like Archbishop Henry, a Minnesota native), borrow $500,000 from Clarence Frame at the First National Bank of St. Paul, with Gerry and other friends guaranteeing the loan's repayment.

"We borrowed the money at something like six or seven percent interest, which was the going rate in the United States at the time, and sent it to Skillingstad at Sogang. Skillingstad invested the money over there at twenty-seven to thirty percent interest and converted enough of the return into dollars to pay the $90,000 per year the Jesuits had been providing. Over the course of the next ten years, Skillingstad wisely invested that money in Korea money markets and had well over a million dollars left over. If there was ever a case of having your cake and eating it, too—well, that was it."

Visiting the Vatican in Rome, both Gerry and Hanky explain, has been an awe-inspiring experience, each of the several times they've gone. The grandeur and beauty of the Vatican itself—especially St. Peter's Cathedral, the magnificent art, and the twenty centuries of church history—almost defies description. Pope John Paul II, whom the Rauenhorsts have met several times, is impressive in his own right. His English is excellent, Hanky has said, "and he looks you directly in the eye when he speaks to you." The experience is not at all intimidating, though, she added. "He's such a kind man, and he makes you feel very comfortable."

Hanky's experience with the Pope may be unique. On one trip to Rome, she had been selected to read the Epistle. On the way to the papal Mass, she stumbled on the ancient sidewalk and fell. "My nose was cut and bleeding, and I didn't even have a BandAid, so I put a little piece of Kleenex on the cut," she would recall. "When we met the Pope after Mass, the Pope said, 'You read very well this morning.' Cardinal [John] O'Connor then pointed to my nose and explained what had happened, and the Pope said, 'Well, I will bless her nose.' So my *nose* received a papal blessing!"

In 1988, Gerry and four other American lay Catholics helped establish the Papal Foundation to raise an endowment the earnings of which would be available for the Pope to use at his discretion. Now the foundation is annually distributing about $3 million for various causes. On a recent papal visit to Cuba, for instance, $100,000 was given to Fidel Castro for the Cuban people. "That impressed me," Gerry said. "Here was the Pope, the head of the Catholic church, reaching out to help the people of a Communist country. The gift made me proud of the work we had done with the Papal Foundation."

Also in 1988, Gerry was one of four laymen who, along with Cardinal John Krol and John O'Connor and Archbishop (now Cardinal) Theodore McCarrick, had breakfast with John Paul in a Vatican dining room. "The Pope was dressed in the white robe you always see him pictured in," as Gerry describes the unusual meeting. "He was on one side of the table with Archbishop McCarrick on one side of him and Cardinal O'Connor on the other. I sat on the opposite side with Cardinal Krol. There was strong Italian coffee served in nice little china cups for everyone but the Pope, who, for some reason, drank his coffee out of a large mug. He obviously enjoyed his coffee. There were also plates of fruit and cold meats. When the meat plate was passed around the table, I was told to be sure to try the Polish sausage!

"Overall, as an individual Catholic, with members of my family, or on church-related business, I've probably met the Pope a dozen times. But, apparently, having breakfast with him was unusual. I feel very honored to have had the chance."

Gerry has met several American presidents over the years, including Ronald Reagan and both Bushes (the younger Bush while he was still governor of Texas). He and Hanky were invited to the elder Bush's home in Kennebunkport, Maine, when Barbara Bush was on the board of the Mayo Clinic and the Rauenhorsts were invited as friends of the clinic. Since then, Gerry has been invited to serve on the advisory council of the Mayo Clinic's president, which Barbara Bush heads. The Rauenhorsts have met high-ranking governmental officials, including several Minnesota senators, representatives, and governors, on various ceremonial, business-related, or personal occasions. But John Paul, they agree, is someone very special.

"He's very personable, very understanding, and very effective," Gerry says. "He speaks excellent English, listens carefully, and has a good sense of humor. I believe that if he were running General Motors, General Motors would be a lot better off as a result. In fact, I believe that he's the most influential man on earth, politically, and am totally convinced he had more to do with bringing down Communism than anybody else in the world. He's a *very* impressive man."

Back at home, Archbishop Harry Flynn, leader of the Archdiocese of St. Paul and Minneapolis, offers his impression of the Rauenhorsts, whom he's come to know well during the past several years:

"Gerry and Hanky are quiet Catholics, people of deep faith. They have created a tremendous example—for their children, who have learned their parents' lessons well, and for so many who will follow after them.

"I'd describe Gerry as a modest man who can walk comfortably both with kings and the common man."

Chapter Five

Opus

"In the late 1960s, I began to think seriously about the future of this company," Gerry told interviewers several years later. "We had as much as thirty percent of the construction market in the Twin Cities. I compared our situation to that of General Motors; if Chevrolet could expect to sell at the most twenty percent of the automobiles bought in this country, how could we expect to attract a greater percentage of our market?

"I realized that we were either going to have to expand geographically or get into other industries here in Minnesota. We were so good at construction, I figured we could do anything else we wanted. With all the brilliant people we had, I thought there would be nothing to it."

But the company's expertise was not as portable as Gerry might have thought. Even the expansion into the shelter and shopping mall markets—basically construction projects with different requirements—proved disappointing.

In 1974, the company commissioned an extensive evaluation by the respected national management-consulting firm McKinsey & Company. Gerry and his executives had decided it was time to take a hard look at their business as it entered its third decade. In the previous five years, the company had expanded and diversified, significantly increased its real estate investments; formed a subsidiary, Fabcon, a prefabricator of concrete walls and floors; ventured into the residential and shopping center markets, and opened an office in Milwaukee (its first outside of the Twin Cities). Most important, perhaps, the tiny firm that had grown out of that little house in Richfield was now a large company—the acorn had become an oak. It was not exactly in the same league as General Motors, but it was surely big enough to think carefully about what it had become and where it now wanted to go.

McKinsey's recommendations?

Stick to the business you know best: construction.

Accelerate your geographic expansion.

Lease space to quality tenants in custom-built buildings.

Cut back your land development and speculative building activity.

Drop your shelter, shopping center, and most other diversification efforts (excepting Fabcon, which was profitable and fit Rauenhorst's construction business).

Replace short-term borrowing with a longer-term financial structure.

"For Gerry," Pine and Mundale wrote, "the [McKinsey] report meant tempering his innate entrepreneurial spirit."

A student of history and human behavior [the historians continued], Gerry had modeled his company's growth on the growth patterns of the companies he admired. "During our formative years, I watched other, more established contractors. Once they became successful in construction, they diversified. It seemed the only way a construction company could succeed. Construction is different from other industries. You can't sell a construction company because it is nothing but people. Two used wheelbarrows—and you're in the construction business...."

The McKinsey study not only affected the corporation's diversification philosophy, but also its management style. The study suggested it was time to move from an entrepreneurial management approach, with its shoot-from-the-hip risk-taking and inherent spontaneity, to a professional management approach, with the attendant hierarchies and chains of command. This new approach meant that Gerry would have to give up some control of the decision-making process....

In September 1974, the company announced consolidation into two divisions—Construction, to be run by Nick Simons, and Real Estate, under Bob Dahlin. The restructuring included the elimination of the firm's shelter operations and curtailment of shopping center development, and brought emerging leaders like Keith Bednarowski (who had managed the Milwaukee office) into important headquarters positions.

"These changes have been made after a great deal of study and concern," Gerry told employees at the time. "I personally feel that the Rauenhorst Corporation will be a stronger, happier, more efficient organization in the future as a result of these actions."

A Visionary's Vision

By that time, Gerry and his team were ensconced on the twenty-second and twenty-third floors of the Northwestern Financial Center they had built on the south side of Interstate 494 in Bloomington. Gerry had high hopes of making the tower's twenty-fourth floor a posh revolving restaurant, but that's a plan that never saw the light of day. Actually, the building leased so quickly it didn't need a restaurant to attract tenants; despite some tentative negotiations with a prominent local restaurateur, the NFC's top floor became home base instead to the well-known Larkin Hoffman law firm.

In his mind's eye, if not with the literal help of the 100-power telescope he kept in his office, Gerry could take in a constellation of substantial projects that, by the mid-seventies, included industrial parks in Eagan and Woodbury, in the eastern and southeastern Twin Cities metro area; Bismarck's 410,000-square-foot Kirkwood Plaza, the largest shopping center in both Dakotas; a Control Data Corporation plant on the distressed North Side of Minneapolis, where Gerry committed his company to hiring contractors and laborers from the neighborhood's minority community; and major components of the so-called "new town" of Jonathan, a work-and-living community located southwest of Minneapolis in the outer-ring suburb of Chaska. Rauenhorst Construction was one of the 200 top contractors in the country, according to *Engineering News Record*.

Framed documents on his office walls reminded him (if he needed reminding) of many personal honors and achievements, among them Marquette University's Alumnus of the Year Award and memberships in the Young President's Association, Society of Civil Engineers, and Minnesota Society of Professional Engineers. Not so visible perhaps but at least as meaningful was the initiation of the company's 1/40 Program and Progress Valley, and his growing advisory and fundraising roles on behalf of Marquette, St. Thomas, and Sogang College in Korea.

There was also, no doubt, the satisfaction that followed the launch of a venture capital group, Northstar Ventures, and the rescue, as part of a ten-man group of local investors, of Twin Cities-based International Dairy Queen. That company became very successful and, in 2002, would be sold to Warren Buffett's Berkshire Hathaway organization for $700 million.

(As an IDQ investor, Gerry came to know its CEO, Mike Sullivan. Impressed with Mike's judgment and management style, Gerry eventually asked Mike to join the Opus board, where, in Gerry's words, "he's been invaluable, because he levels with us, tells it like it is, and brings an objective outsider's perspective.")

Gerry turned forty-seven in the waning days of 1974 and was by then well-established in the construction and development industry, the local philanthropic community, the Catholic church in America, and, importantly, among the corporate leadership of his adopted home-town. Board memberships, in fact, had provided him, early on, with essential mentors (such as Henry Rutledge and Clarence Frame), a powerful education in corporate management and governance, and influential connections with like-minded civic leaders and philanthropists.

He would choose his board memberships as carefully as the boards chose him, believing that each could teach him something he felt he needed to know in order to grow and improve his own business. On the Peavey board, for instance, Gerry observed how a longtime family company operates after selling its stock to the public. On the ConAgra board, he learned how a radically decentralized company works. And on Northwestern Bell's board, how a subsidiary performs within a holding company. Such experiences provided him invaluable perspective as Opus decentralized into regional operations.

Yet another valuable perspective was afforded by Gerry's association with Deutschebank, the Germany-based international financial giant. Gerry had been doing business with Deutschebank in New York during the 1980s and had become friendly with Dr. Rolf Breuer, the future CEO of the company. The German firm had started a REIT that owned three properties in North America: an insurance company facility in Seattle, a bank tower in Denver, and the Norwest Bank building in Minneapolis.

"Dr. Breuer, the number-two man in Europe, asked me to join the board of that [real estate investment trust—REIT]," Gerry says. "Well, I thought it was a good chance for me to learn more about Europe and enhance our relationship with Deutschebank, which at that time was one of the largest, if not the largest, bank outside the United States. So I joined, and over the course of seven or eight years made several trips to New York and Europe—wherever the board meetings were held. I'd fly overnight to London, if that's where the meeting was scheduled, arrive at nine in the morning, attend the meeting until three in the afternoon, then catch a four o'clock flight back to the U.S. It was really quite convenient, and I never got out of sync because I've always been able to sleep well on airplanes.

"Anyway, I remained on that board until they were listed on the New York Stock Exchange and became independent. By that time I felt I had learned all I could from the situation and thought I should channel that time elsewhere."

An interesting footnote: "I was chairman of the Norwest Bank Corporation board's finance committee when the Northwestern Financial Center was built and it was proposed to sell the building to a particular REIT," Gerry says. "I didn't know until later that that was the REIT I'd eventually join as a director."

Such experiences taught Gerry valuable lessons that he has applied to the structuring and operation of his own board. Mike Sullivan, the Opus director whom Gerry met through his aforementioned Dairy Queen involvement, has served on several corporate boards; he calls Opus "a textbook model for running a private family company. Gerry and the Opus management realize that people outside the company can contribute to change. They listen carefully. They are not ingrown."

For that matter, Gerry's fellow board members, as well as sundry other local business leaders with whom he had become familiar, were learning a lot from, and about, Gerry. In a lengthy profile that appeared in the *Minneapolis Tribune* in 1974, several of those individuals shared their impressions.

Walter Nelson, then president of the Eberhardt Company, a real estate sales and brokerage company: "He's unusually hard-working, and he doesn't procrastinate. He's very candid and he's willing to take the big chance, but he takes it after careful investigation and deliberation. He's an unassuming guy, and I suppose that leads some people to believe that he's unsophisticated and naive. Maybe that's one reason why he does so well, because he's neither."

Jim Curry, who with Ed Dunn, developed Pentagon Park: "I really think he's the Henry Kissinger of the local real estate world. He finds out what the parties want and goes from there. In a quiet sort of way, he's the most powerful man I've known. If you make waves by doing your job well and often, pretty soon waves are made for you. People expect him to win now, and he does.

"He's powerful in what he represents, and so he deals from strength. Losing simply isn't a viable alternative."

Robert Engels, chairman and CEO of Northern States Power Company: "I think that Gerry conscientiously believes that he's a steward of what the Lord has given him."

But looking out from his perch atop the NFC tower at the end of 1974, what likely most drew Gerry's long gaze—and fired his imagination—were the first signs of the new project the company had dubbed Opus 2, at the junction of Highway 18 and the Crosstown highway in Minnetonka just west of Minneapolis. (There would be no *Opus 1*—which existed only briefly, on paper, as a development planned for the east side of the Twin Cities, or, in any form, *Opus 3*. There would be only *Opus 2* and, of course, *Opus Corporation*, the name the company chose for itself in 1982.)

Opus 2 was something the visionary Gerry Rauenhorst had been "seeing" for several years, even when others couldn't. In 1972, he described that vision, and its context, in the company's newsletter:

It seems to me that we are spending the largest amounts of government funds in places where the majority of the people don't want to live. This leads me to wonder if more of our development efforts shouldn't be in building the right kind of community for all socioeconomic categories of people where the majority of them would like to live—in the suburbs. Most of our suburban developments have been on a piecemeal basis, with an occasional planned unit development.

In the Twin Cities there are still areas where as many as 500 to 1,000 acres could be assembled within six or eight miles of the cities' centers. I envision the development of a total unit that would house some 15,000 people, with enough office, industrial, and commercial space to employ 2,000 to 3,000. Forty percent or more of the area could be left for parks, greenways, and recreation facilities, and the balance could be developed to a higher density than is now the case.

Gerry believed the development could reduce the need for expensive transportation. It could contain two roadway systems—one for conventional automobiles, the other limited to pedestrian and bicycle traffic and "small electric cars with a maximum speed of fifteen miles per hour...."

"It is my hope," Gerry concluded, "that someday soon the Rauenhorst Corporation will be involved in a development that would incorporate many of the above ideas. The ultimate result could be a better way of life for all segments of American society."

Gerry had already broached his idea to a handful of friends and associates, including Bob Dahlin (who was not yet working for the Rauenhorst Corporation). Dahlin heard Gerry talk about buying land on Highway 18 near the Crosstown and building a "complete community, residential and commercial, and with buried utilities right from the start... a planned community where people could both work and live."

Dahlin told him it was a "crazy idea" and advised him to forget it.

Eventually, however, Gerry found a sympathetic ear in Ed Orenstein, president and CEO of Data 100, a locally based maker of computer terminals. Like Gerry, Orenstein was concerned about the distances Americans in general and his own employees in particular were commuting between home and work. (For personal reasons, Orenstein was keen on having the company's new headquarters situated within a five-minute drive of his Edina home.) In any event, Orenstein said that Data 100 would be the first occupant of Opus 2, on the more than 300 acres of erstwhile farmland that Gerry and George Connor were beginning to buy at the Minnetonka site.

By the end of 1973, ground had been broken, and Gerry's vision was beginning to be a reality.

Opus 2

During Opus 2's planning and construction, the "crazy" development was never far from Gerry's mind, even as the company continued to consolidate and reorganize, began to expand geographically, including, via its Milwaukee office, in the Chicago suburbs, and embarked on several important—and remarkably diverse—new projects, including the Halfaer Recreation Center at Marquette University, parts of the Valleyfair amusement park south of Minneapolis, the fourteen-story First National Bank Building in Billings (at the time the tallest building in Montana), and the American State Bank in Olivia (the company's first project in Gerry's hometown since the Zion

Lutheran Church in 1953). Gerry's children remember him laying out Opus 2's unusual one-way road system using colored ribbons on at least one occasion while he was supposedly relaxing at the lake.

John Albers was a young architect at the time, not long out of the University of Minnesota, recently hired by the firm, and eager to make a contribution. One Saturday morning, Albers drove out to the Opus 2 site to get a feel for the lay of the land literally and figuratively both. As he walked along the southern edge of the as-yet-undeveloped, otherwise deserted property, he was surprised to be joined, out of the blue, by another man who was busy looking over the site as well.

"It was Gerry," Albers recalls. "He wanted to look at the site, too. I remember thinking, 'What are the odds? It's a Saturday and I'm here checking things out, and who should appear but the boss himself.' Of course, I'm also thinking, 'Well, this is a good way for the new guy to make a favorable impression'—but I'm also just happy he's here and we're both interested in the same thing. It was a very nice feeling, the two of us out there like that."

Finally, in September 1977, Gerry presided over Opus 2's grand opening. "Ceremonies included presentation of a deed for forty-nine acres of park space to the mayor of Minnetonka," according to company records. "The development received citations for engineering excellence from the Consulting Engineers Council of Minnesota, [which] praised the careful preservation of the Opus landscape and the unique system of roads, trails, and bridges." Earlier that year, Data Card Corporation had become part of the development, in the form of a $3.3 million international headquarters building. In other news, because Rauenhorst had withdrawn from the shelter market as part of its reorganization, the company had sold Opus 2's residential tracts to other developers.

In 1978, with Opus 2 up and running, the company celebrated its silver anniversary.

In a quarter of a century, the company had logged more than 670 building projects totaling more than $400 million [management reported]. The distinctive Rauenhorst logo could be seen in twelve states from Montana to New Jersey and from Cloquet, Minnesota, to Dallas, Texas. Rauenhorst had truly grown with the suburbs; more than 2,000 people worked in Opus 2 alone. The company was nearing completion of Shady Oak Office Center, an 85,000-square-foot building [at Opus 2] to be co-owned with Aetna Life Insurance Company. Opus 2 also included a regional office center for American Family Insurance Group and the Upper Midwest Trade Center, an exhibition hall for the Upper Midwest Allied Gifts Association.

By 1978, Rauenhorst had underway $67 million in design/build projects. It owned 450 acres of land that could be developed...and it managed three-million square feet of office space. By the end of the year, the company had revenues of $91.7 million—revenues that had more than doubled in the past four years. At the same time, Progress Valley...was a thriving charitable enterprise, and the corporation decided to begin Progress Valley II, a halfway house for women.

The company was deeply involved in a three-phase marketing development plan that would take nearly three-and-a-half years to complete.... To back up its design/build reputation, Rauenhorst had strengthened its design department, [which now] included eleven architects, seven engineers, and twelve draftsmen. With full structural and mechanical capabilities, Rauenhorst had to contract outside the company only for electrical engineering services.

In another phase of its reorganization, the company created a chief operating officer's position, to direct day-to-day operations, freeing Gerry —after more than twenty-five years of daily operating responsibility—to focus on strategy and growth. While Gerry remained chairman and CEO, Bob Dahlin was named company president and COO. That change, and the addition, over the previous few years, of top managers like Gene Haugland and Bill Tobin, testified to the continuing transition from an entrepreneurial company to a professionally managed corporation.

"The person who has organized a firm and personally assumed the risk is often reluctant to relinquish management authority," Gerry wrote in the company newsletter during the spring of 1979, by way of explaining the recent changes at the top. "At some point in a company's development that tight control may have a stifling effect, restraining the development and fulfillment of other capable individuals in the organization and possibly limiting the company's horizons.

"Having observed that phenomenon in a number of companies, I decided this was a good time to broaden the leadership responsibilities at Rauenhorst Corporation."

That year, the company surpassed for the first time the $100-million annual sales mark, signed their two biggest construction jobs to date (National Car Rental's headquarters and a manufacturing plant for Saxon Industries' Brown and Bigelow operation, both in the Twin Cities), and launched studies that would lead to further geographic expansion beyond existing markets in Milwaukee and Chicago to new territory in the U.S. Southwest.

By the end of 1979, the company began work, as part of a joint venture with Aetna Life, on the sixteen-story Southwest Financial Center in Phoenix. The center was quickly followed by a twenty-story tower, also in Phoenix, for Phelps Dodge, the big copper-mining concern. Both buildings were locally praised for their striking appearance, innovative layout, and energy-efficient design. In Mount Prospect, Illinois, meanwhile, the company began work on the 300-acre Kensington Center for Business, and, in Downer's Grove, also near Chicago, broke ground for Continental Can Company's 82,000-square-foot office facility.

The following year, back in Minnetonka, a ten-story tower that would be the centerpiece of Opus 2 was begun, following a collaborative design by Rauenhorst architects and consulting architects from the renowned Boston-based firm Benjamin Thompson & Associates. The new building would become, albeit not without a significant hitch, another landmark for the company.

The 300,000-square-foot Opus Center was intended to be the

international headquarters of the Toro Company, the large Twin Cities-based manufacturer of lawn-care and snow-handling equipment. No one had counted, however, on the vagaries of the weather, which dealt the project a serious blow. As Gerry recounts the situation:

> Toro had leased half the building with options to take the rest. But when we finished it, because of a string of unusually mild winters, Toro had three years of unsold snow blowers in its warehouse and was on the verge of bankruptcy. Furthermore, not long after the lease was signed, Dave McLaughlin, Toro's CEO, had left the company to become president of Dartmouth College.
>
> Steve Keating, a Toro board member and highly respected former president of Honeywell, Inc., had taken over, and he came to see me about our common problem. By this time, Toro had been paying the rent and trying, to no avail, to sublease the Opus Center space for nine months, and Steve said in effect, "Gerry, we've got to get rid of this lease or we'll go bankrupt. I've worked things out with the banks, and if we can get rid of the lease they'll give us the financing to keep going. We can pay you $3 million to cancel the lease. In fact, I've got the check right here."
>
> Well, I thought about the situation for a minute or two and then decided that we should get on with life. I said, "Steve, you're a real gentleman. I believe this is your best offer, so I'll take the check. You're off the lease." He thanked me, and we shook hands. I said, "I'll call our lawyer and we'll record the receipt of your check." He said, "Oh, don't worry about that. We can take care of it later." And he left—leaving me with a check for $3 million! I thought, "There's a classy fellow, and that's a perfect example of Minnesota Nice!"

After working out a satisfactory termination of Toro's lease obligation, the Rauenhorst group moved its headquarters into the new building, the sixth since the company's founding. In addition, at Steve Keating's urging, Honeywell agreed to lease almost 37,000 square feet to use as a training center and human-resources department. "This proved again," says Gerry, "what a fine gentleman Steve was."

In yet another significant development in 1982, Rauenhorst Corporation officially changed its name to Opus Corporation.

Speaking of the several major adjustments of the previous few years, Gerry wrote at the time, "These changes have given the company a personality and character that have matured beyond those of its founder. It is fitting and logical that the company should now have an identity of its own."

Expanding, Dealing, Decentralizing

By the early eighties, there had been several other developments—not necessarily of the brick-and-mortar variety—that would add luster to and have long-term consequences for the firm.

In 1980, Gerry was one of five Minnesota entrepreneurs named to the state's Business Hall of Fame, along with Alan Ruvelson, president of First Midwest Corporation and First Midwest Capital Corporation in Minneapolis; Reiko Weston, founder of the Fuji-Ya restaurant in Minneapolis; William Marvin, president of Marvin Windows of Warroad; and Raymond Plank, chairman of Apache Corporation of Minneapolis.

On February 1, 1982, the two newly formed trusts for the Rauenhorst children and grandchildren each bought one-half of the assets of Dyson & Company. The venerable, sixty-one-year-old construction firm, based in Pensacola, Florida, had operations in five southeastern states. Rauenhorst opened a branch office in Tampa, where Keith Bednarowski presided over the subsequently renamed Dyson Company. According to an earlier corporate account, the merger was "the result of several years' planning" by the Rauenhorst team.

> The company's managers began to see that the construction industry was gradually moving from a union-dominated work force to a non-union one. "We saw that less union construction was occurring overall, and that most construction was occurring in parts

of the country that were dominated by non-union companies," says Jim Mullin [then the company's senior vice president for planning]. "We realized that if Opus were to continue to grow, it had to have a strong presence in right-to-work states and to compete effectively as a non-union contractor. We believed that the best way to do that was to acquire an existing non-union company whose reputation and field crew were already established."

Furthermore, Mullin says, "another operation in corporate form was useful to the long-term estate plan recommended to Gerry by his legal and tax divisions."

Nineteen-eighty-two additionally marked the entrance into the firm of the grown-up second generation of Rauenhorsts.

Judy, Gerry and Hanky's oldest child, had worked in sales and promotion at Control Data's Peripheral Products Company, in Control Data's public relations department, and as director of public information at the State of Minnesota's Department of Economic Development when she joined the marketing department of her father's firm.

Mark, their oldest son, had cut his teeth as the head of the human resources department at the Minnesota plant of American Linen Supply, then, after earning an MBA with a concentration in finance at Notre Dame, was treasury services manager (in charge of corporate investments and pension and retirement plans) at Graco Company. At twenty-nine, he joined Opus, working initially in finance, sales, and asset management. Three years later he moved into property management and was put in charge of Normandale Properties.

Second son Neil, an architect who had worked at Skidmore, Owings & Merrill in Chicago, joined Opus's Windy City office to work in real estate development.

So, for the first time since Hanky "retired" to raise their children, the company was, operationally, truly a family business. The proud parents couldn't have been happier.

In the meantime, on the local construction front, Opus built its first building—the twenty-three-floor office tower known by its address, 100 South Fifth Street—in downtown Minneapolis. "This was not a building designed to blend unobtrusively into the downtown skyline," a corporate observer reported. "The top five floors [were] built in a curved and stepped arrangement, opening up sky-level space for greenhouses and open-air patios. The southeast corner of the building's lot would be landscaped as a plaza, with trees and greenery amid the surrounding concrete and glass. Before 100 South Fifth was completed, Gerry would announce a unique 'joint venture' with the Minneapolis Institute of Arts to provide an outdoor display space for sculpture. Named 'Sculpture Square,' the space would be used as the setting for a series of large works owned by the Institute."

The downtown structure, completed in 1984, drew admiring comments from a range of appreciative citizens and "experts," including Bernard Jacob writing in *Architecture Minnesota* magazine and the *Star Tribune's* woman-about-town, Barbara Flanagan. The latter quoted Opus's chief architect, John Albers, saying that "he wanted to [produce] a design that is elegant, urban, and yet 'very Minnesotan'"—which, it certainly was. "The glass skyways are his idea and so is the decision to route the skyway around the outside edge of the building instead of through the middle," Flanagan noted approvingly. A second, complementary office tower—150 South Fifth—was soon built next door, and Opus was, for the first time, a significant presence in the commercial heart of its own hometown.

"For thirty years, Opus had built in the suburbs and drawn most of its tenants out of downtown," Gerry reflected years later. "In the early eighties, however, it became apparent that the Twin Cities' downtowns were starting to revive.

"Because I had a close association with Northwestern Bell—I was on their board—I had become interested in a piece of property they owned in downtown Minneapolis. So we formed a joint venture with them to build 100 South Fifth Street. The building was very successful, and we sold it to LaSalle Real Estate of Chicago in 1986. That was an example of how well things had been going for us during the early and mid-eighties.

"I looked around at the time and saw that we were selling buildings for far more than it cost us to build them," Gerry continued. "We owned, by ourselves or with partners, twenty-seven high-rise buildings across America, and we could reproduce all of them for probably seventy percent of their sale price. So I said to my officers, 'This is stupid. Why don't we sell them and build more like them?' So we set out, in 1986, to sell those twenty-seven buildings and, by 1989, had sold twenty of them.

"In the meantime, we built 150 South Fifth. Then our partner, Northwestern Bell, needed some cash and wanted to sell. (A typical public company problem: They were a little short that quarter.) So they asked us to take them out of the partnership, which we did, in the process of putting on a convertible mortgage with the same company that bought 100 South Fifth. We had a 'put' three years hence. Well, in three years, that building was worth about seventy percent of the convertible mortgage and obviously we 'put' it to them. I still remember watching those lawyers from Chicago coming into our board room with dour faces, having to buy a building they didn't want but were obligated to buy for a price beyond what it was worth three years later."

Further organizational changes were, meantime, under way. Bob Dahlin retired as company president and became vice chairman in 1984; he was succeeded as president by Bill Tobin. The same year, Nick Simons, one of Gerry's most valued associates for almost twenty-five years, decided to retire. Then, in 1988, Tobin left Opus. Dahlin came out of retirement to be chairman and CEO of the newly minted Opus U.S. Corporation, with Keith Bednarowski becoming president and chief operating officer. Gerry remained chairman and CEO of a sister company, Opus Corporation, with Gene Haugland as president and COO.

That same year, Opus U.S., under the leadership of Dahlin and Bednarowski, crafted the decentralization model that pushed responsibility and authority into well-defined regions and branch offices and became a hallmark of the company's current success. Neil Rauenhorst became president of the Opus South region. Jim Nygard was named president of Opus North. Opus Southwest was formed under president George Mikesh.

"In essence," Gerry had explained to his employees at the time of the reorganization in the 1980s, "this is a major change in the way we operate. We are going to have four smaller operations—North, South, Southwest, and Minneapolis—with a unified head, rather than one large operation with two divisions. Construction and real estate people in each division will report to the manager of that division. [The managers] will be responsible for the bottom line in their division, rather than at the corporate level."

On the larger subject of effective organization, he said:

> I believe that the most difficult problem in management is to delegate authority and responsibility in large and equal amounts. If you give someone a lot of authority and no responsibility, that person will become a dictator. If you give a lot of responsibility and no authority, that person becomes a slave. I believe you can delegate authority and responsibility in large, equal amounts.
>
> I have seen others in this industry who have not been willing to give up either responsibility or authority. They run their businesses with a telephone at each ear, talking at the same time to two or three people in the room. They make *every* decision about the business—right down to negotiating ten cents a foot more on a lease. In their businesses, every employee is something of a slave because so little authority is delegated. And it isn't responsibility but authority that makes work enjoyable.
>
> People work better when they feel that what they're doing is theirs. The more you leave them alone, let them run their show, the better they like it.
>
> When the McKinsey people came to study us in 1974, they gave me a booklet describing what they called "threshold companies"—companies at a stage when they must cease being entrepreneurial and become professionally managed corporations. I read that book carefully, and I decided I had better make the transition. The McKinsey report confirmed that the path of authority and responsibility was the right way to go, and that we should stay on it.

Various Perspectives

The changes did not go unnoticed in the places Rauenhorst/Opus did business. Typical of the commentary during the period was an admiring profile that ran in the *St. Paul Pioneer Press* in 1981, three years *before* the geographic decentralization was announced. That story read in part:

> Rauenhorst's strong belief in the individual carries over into his approach to management. He runs a highly decentralized operation, encouraging each manager of the company's six divisions—construction, real estate, accounting, design, field, and legal—to take on responsibility by making their own decisions.
>
> "We want people to make the decisions on the lowest level possible. It's a discipline. It keeps the red tape out and the people motivated and challenged."
>
> "Gerry is the supreme manager," said Robert A. Worthington, director of planning and governmental affairs. "He knows how to motivate people without directly managing. That's the biggest compliment that any person could get. He's saying I believe in you—you're my future...."

Despite the corporate name change and his reduction of day-to-day operational management, Gerry was getting more personal attention than ever. As heralded by his election to the state's Business Hall of Fame at the beginning of the decade, he was, after thirty years in business, one of the region's better known and most admired leaders, at least within the regional business community.

Interestingly, however, for a man so straightforward and direct, he created some decidedly, almost comically diverse impressions among his contemporaries and the local media.

In a long, effusive cover story, editor Charles Mundale described *Corporate Report* magazine's 1983 Executive of the Year like this:

> If Gerald Rauenhorst built automobiles, he would probably

build automobiles like the gray Mercedes 380 SL he drives. If Mercedes-Benz built men (a more remote prospect), the conservative, quality-conscious German firm would probably build men like Gerald Rauenhorst.

Rauenhorst's snugly tailored suit, his wrinkle-free shirt, and a tie that hangs as straight as a plumb line reflect the same Teutonic discipline that controls the understated lines of this sleek sedan....

Unfortunately for the American automobile industry, Gerald Rauenhorst does not build cars. He builds buildings, and—fortunately for Minnesota—most of the 846 he has built in the past thirty years are right here in his home state. They have not always had the elegance of a Mercedes, but neither has their builder. The meticulous haberdashery of the man and rapidly improving architecture of his buildings have been—like the Mercedes' fenders—a late, congruent addition to the basic product....

Dick Youngblood, one of the Twin Cities' sharpest business commentators, made the following observations about Gerry and Opus, in a *Minneapolis Tribune* column in 1984:

The sprawling office with its Honduran mahogany paneling and marble fireplace doesn't look anything like a casino. And the slender man behind the bulky eighteenth-century mahogany desk wears the pinstriped uniform of the business executive, not the sleeve garters of the blackjack dealer.

"We don't have to go to Las Vegas to gamble," said Gerald Rauenhorst.

Indeed. Consider, for example, the imposing Opus Center ...that Rauenhorst's Opus Corporation calls home. Rauenhorst built the ten-story...complex on speculation, but with assurances that the high-flying Toro Company would use a substantial chunk of it as a corporate headquarters.

By the time the $20 million building opened in 1982, however,

Toro's snowblower business had stumbled badly because of several unsnowy winters. Toro bought out of its lease, leaving Rauenhorst with a gaping space to fill—and a substantial debt to service.

Two years later the center is 85 percent leased. More important, it is one of five Opus-owned buildings around the country in which the General Motors Pension Fund bought a half-interest last month.

The price: "Well in excess of $100 million," Rauenhorst said.

In Rauenhorst's league, in short, Las Vegas would be the minors. For Opus Corporation, a design, construction, and development firm, assumes full risk on most of its projects, using its revolving credit line to bankroll a development and counting on its own expertise to market the results successfully....

"Our objective is to put up the best building for the least amount of money," he said. "We figure the coordination between design and construction can save us 10 to 15 percent on building costs." And involvement of Opus's building-management professionals in the design and construction process, he added, can produce a 10 to 20 percent saving on energy and other operating costs.

In thirty-one years in the industry, Rauenhorst has translated this strategy into a business that should produce revenues of about $175 million in 1984, up 17 percent from $150 million last year and four times the level of just a decade ago....

Today, Opus manages seventy-four properties containing 7 million square feet of space in a dozen metropolitan areas across the country. The company owns all or part of the majority of them, and 1 million square feet of new space will be opened in the next twelve to sixteen months....

Three years later, another local journalist, Sharon Schmickle, writing in the *Star Tribune*, described Gerry in *these* terms:

Rauenhorst is a blue-suited corporate executive in a field of riverboat gamblers. Amid high-flying risk takers, he is controlled, methodical, and purposeful. Other developers scramble to assemble deals; he has slowly built a corporation that builds buildings with a full-service approach that is unusual in the industry.

Rauenhorst's business dealings reflect the man: immaculate in his trim business suits, dead direct in his gaze, conservative in his politics, constructive in his community activities, and principled in his personal affairs....

He avoids the limelight that other developers crave.

Rauenhorst's companies have created more than 1,000 buildings. In recent years, the operation has completed more than $200 million worth of construction annually, enough to make the top 100 in *Engineering News-Record's* rankings of the nation's 400 leading contractors.

None of the buildings bears the name Rauenhorst.

"If I found one that did, I'd take it off," he said....

Many of Gerry's peers in the local business community had their own opinions, often reflecting their concerns about critical organizational matters such as corporate culture. In 1984, Bill Reiling, then president of Twin Cities-based Towle Real Estate Company, observed, for instance:

[When he started] Gerry Rauenhorst didn't have a fifty-year-old culture that dictated the way things had always been done, like so many construction companies in this area. He could try something new—pulling all the pieces of a new building together for a customer. He could say, "We'll design a building that satisfies you and meets your budget. We'll find a site, if one of the fifteen or twenty [sites] we have right now isn't right. When the building is finished, you can own it for this much, lease it at this rate, or lease with an option to buy. We'll take care of everything—you just tell us what you want."

He made Opus a *market-driven* company. He provides the customer with a building based on the customer's needs. Opus sells a concept, not a building. The company doesn't have to compete on price, because it is selling so much more.

Not that Opus's progress was ever a steady climb or unbroken series of successes. There were good years and better years—and, if only occasionally, a few patches coinciding with national dips and recessions that weren't very uplifting at all.

In the late seventies and early eighties, when the company entertained the notion of becoming, in Gerry's words, "a mini-conglomerate," management bought several and sundry enterprises that could now charitably be said to have "seemed a good idea at the time." Perhaps most memorable of the clunkers was a manufacturer that had a unique machine that very efficiently stamped out plastic products such as bath tubs, kitchen sinks, and canoes. The manager of the plastics company was a former Sears executive who had received a large order from the giant retailer subject to the retailer's approval. As Gerry recounts the next step, "Then somebody at Sears dumped something you might expect to dump into a sink into one of the plastic company's sample products—and the bottom promptly melted and fell out." So much for the big Sears order, and so much for the plastics firm itself. All that remained of that business a few months later was a plastic canoe that Gerry keeps at his lake retreat as a reminder of those times. He calls it his "million-dollar canoe."

Sometimes it wasn't internal miscalculations but the vagaries of the national economy that created the headaches. "From 1989 until about 1992 or '93, we struggled," Gerry conceded in a 1994 interview. "Phoenix went from forty-one people in the office down to thirteen people. The company had never had a major layoff before. Now we had to terminate people with as much as twenty years' experience. That was a lot of good people, but we had to do that to survive. [The market] was really down to nothing. Where you used to go into a city and see twenty tower cranes, now you saw none. As we joked at the time, 'The yellow tower crane is extinct!' We did pick up work here and there. We went out and did government work. We won competitions in Washington and California. We won three out of four competitions that we entered. We could be very competitive because of our vertical integration and our ability to put it all together."

More recently, Gerry looked back on the same dicey period to make the following observations:

"In 1989, the industry went over a cliff. It was not a descent. It was a free fall. You could not sell anything. You could not lease anything. The banks were calling in loans. I would guess that if eighty percent of our competitors didn't file bankruptcy, it was only because of the grace of their lenders. But during that entire time we paid every bank debt, interest, and principal on time. We'd done that throughout our history, and we did it then, even in those tough times. We sold a lot of properties at prices we didn't like, but we did so to preserve our record and reputation of never defaulting, of never missing a payment.

"Another important point: We've long operated according to the FIFO—first in, first out—principle. Now I know that's an accounting term, but how we use it has nothing to do with accounting. What we're talking about is anticipating the business cycle. It's not exactly rocket science. For instance, when we'd see office-building vacancy rates falling to five percent, we'd put up a spec building, knowing that in due course there would be a need for it. That's 'first in.' By the same token, if the vacancy rates for some of our buildings would be climbing to twenty percent, we'd sell those first—'first out.'

"We build six different categories of buildings: offices, warehouses, factories, institutions, retail, and residential (condominiums and apartments). Whatever we see there's going to be a need for, that's what we try to build, rather than just adding to what's already there. The way we're organized and deployed, we have more flexibility than virtually any developer I can think of. We can move on a dime, and build almost anything, quickly and efficiently.

"In the late eighties, when office-building vacancies were climbing to twenty percent, one market that wasn't overbuilt was retail. At one point, I was trying to reach my executives and their secretaries were telling me they were in Las Vegas. I thought, 'What the heck is going on here?'

Well, it turned out that seventeen of our executives were at a big international convention of shopping-center people in Vegas. The following year, we had thirty-four of our people at the same convention and a big booth where we were signing up businesses. And, within a couple of years, about fifty percent of our total business was in retail.

"If we don't know a lot about a market we want to move into, we'll find a partner who knows the market but may lack the financing and the other abilities that we have. Our aim is to learn from knowledgeable people until we can do something well ourselves. But that's been one of the major strengths of Opus over the years: We're quick learners and can move in any direction. We're never stuck trying to sell something people don't want."

Opus (like the Rauenhorst Corporation before it) has been consistently lean and light on its feet, and when its founder has taken risks (as per Dick Youngblood et al.), they have been *manageable* risks. If he was in fact a gambler, Gerry was always aware of how much he could afford to lose. So, when private-sector development slumped in the early 1990s, Opus diversified into several high-profile public facility projects, such as the Mariucci hockey arena on the Minneapolis campus of the University of Minnesota and those state office buildings in California and Washington.

"This new line of business, coupled with other moves by the company, has helped see it through some of the worst dog days in memory for both Opus and its industry," Dave Beal wrote, in January 1994, in a *St. Paul Pioneer Press* article headlined, "New Focus for Opus." "The company expects to roughly double the space it has under development this year, compared to 1993. And over the longer haul, Opus seems much better equipped to survive the inescapable downturns that bedevil the industry." The move into the public arena was, in Beal's words, "a sea of change" for Opus, which, nonetheless was suitably adaptable for the times. "For decades, the company shunned such jobs, fearing entanglement with cumbersome public bureaucracies. Or, as Gerry Rauenhorst put it, 'We used to do a government building about once every five years, just to make sure we didn't want to do another one.'"

Beal quoted the head of the State of California's real estate operations saying about Opus, "They came into this community as a relatively unknown company [and] took on the major experienced competitors in Sacramento. Since then, we have had a chance to be working with them for almost a year, and I have found them to be the most cooperative, reasonable, and easy-to-get-along-with group of people that I've ever encountered in the real estate industry. They are so down-to-earth and honest and patient. They're good."

As the company moved into the nineties, it continued its careful strategic restructuring. In 1991, Bob Dahlin retired and Keith Bednarowski became CEO and president. His job was to complete the decentralization of the company under the Opus U.S. banner. Mark Rauenhorst became president and chief operating officer in April 1999. The following year he'd become CEO and president. At the same time, Bednarowski ascended to the office of chairman and Gerry assumed the honorary title of founding chairman. Such was Opus's leadership when the company celebrated its fiftieth anniversary on April 22, 2003.

In 1993, the company had celebrated its fortieth anniversary. The previous year, Opus had been honored as National Developer of the Year by the National Association of Industrial and Office Properties. Three years later, *National Real Estate Investor* magazine named it the top developer in the United States.

In the fall of 1993, Craig Shutt, writing in *Ascent*, a construction-industry publication, observed:

> Few firms have demonstrated the versatility and survival skills shown by Opus Corporation...in the past decade. Its operating divisions include firms involved in property development, asset management, property management, architectural design, engineering, and construction—disciplines that have not exactly thrived in recent years. Yet the firm has found a way to roll with the punches and land on its feet every time.
>
> "Our success has been dependent on our making the right financial decisions about when to get into a project and when to

get out," says John W. Albers, president of architecture and engineering for the firm. Keith Bednarowski agrees. "Our strength today, frankly, is that we have a lot of capital available to us, so we don't need to go to lending institutions to fund the equity for projects."

That situation came about, he adds, for three reasons: the firm sold a lot of properties between 1986 and 1989, as the market began to soften; it stopped doing its own speculative buildings; and it retained its pragmatic approach to the market....

As late as 1985, Albers says, as much as 80 percent of the company's business was done in-house on speculation for the development departments. Today, he estimates that as much as 95 percent of the firm's business is done for third-party customers on a contract basis. "The market has changed, and we changed with it."

Teamwork and Integrity

"Our principal resource is the talent of our employees," said Bill Tobin during a management meeting back in 1984.

Tobin, of course, was repeating a truth that everybody who has worked for the company before and since has had the opportunity to understand and appreciate. The Christmas parties (with bonuses and gifts) dating back to Hanky's home-cooked dinners in the Rauenhorsts' Richfield dining room, the presentation of Christmas hams, the summer picnics and celebrations, and the silver dollar given to each employee on his or her employment anniversary (culminating with a special gold piece on the employee's twenty-fifth anniversary) all speak, in turn, to the company's understanding and appreciation of the hard work, integrity, and loyalty of its employees.

The company has emphasized teamwork since—well, for as long as there's been a *team*. As Mark Rauenhorst once told an interviewer, using the company's real estate deals as an example, "The team trust has to be there. Because every deal is different, the attorneys have to be willing to try something new; so do the finance people; so do the real estate developers. They have to be able to trust the others to do their jobs. That trust and confidence allows individuals to be more creative, and their creative solution can find support.

"Our attitude is that if something goes wrong, let's take a quick look to see what we can learn, but let's not dwell on it," Mark went on. "Because we do operate as a team, the person who might have been responsible isn't isolated. Individuals know that the company is going to stand behind them and their work."

Employees at all levels have historically been invited to share the elation of major accomplishments with management. Old-timers still talk about the parties Gerry and Hanky hosted following the construction of the Howard Johnson hotel and Camelot restaurant in Bloomington back in the sixties.

Post-construction celebrations have often included the company's subcontractors as well. As Nick Simons recalled, "When Rauenhorst completed the Northwestern Financial Center [in 1974], all the laborers and plumbers and electricians were brought together and told how we appreciated their willingness to work as a team. Then we invited the presidents of all the subcontracting companies to the Decathlon Club for lunch, where we told them how much we appreciated *their* cooperation. We also invited all of our foremen and their wives and other people in the company who had worked hard on the project to a wild-game dinner."

At the same time, much has been expected of Rauenhorst/Opus employees, top to bottom, from the beginning. Since 1991, the company has published a formal Code of Conduct to which every Opus director, officer, and employee must subscribe. Its introduction declares:

> The principles that have guided the growth and development of the Opus companies reflect the integrity, moral character, and ethical standards of its founder. The application of these principles in the conduct of our business throughout its history has evolved an "Opus culture," which has produced a reputation of honesty, integrity, and quality.
>
> Opus will endure and prosper by continuing to build on those

principles and practices that have served it well. Each employee is a custodian of its reputation. The Code of Conduct was developed to uniformly convey the guiding principles and core values of Opus, which we ask all employees to endorse, embrace, and embody in all business practices. The Code also reaffirms our commitment to the highest standards of ethical and professional conduct, and offers guidance in making decisions on behalf of Opus. No guidelines can be all-inclusive, however, and the responsibility for maintaining proper conduct rests with each of us. *There is no substitute for personal integrity and good judgment.*

The Code covers everything from conflict of interest and relationships with government officials to interpersonal conduct and accounting systems. Employees must annually review the Code and sign a statement of representation as a condition of employment. Gerry says that living by the Code's tenets is simply "walking the company's talk" about honesty and integrity in both personal and professional behavior.

"I'm proud I could build a business—a family business," he said in a profile that appeared in a University of St. Thomas publication in 1996. "We provide an opportunity for good people to work in an environment where they don't have to compromise their principles. If they did, they wouldn't be here.

"And neither would I."

Chapter Six

Opus Too

"We who design and construct buildings are implementers of physical change to meet evolving needs," Gerry said in a speech almost twenty years ago. He could have said the same thing when he started his business fifty years ago—or, for that matter, when he got out of bed this morning.

As this is written, in the summer of 2003, the Opus Group, most visible of Gerry's many constructions, comprises five horizontally and vertically integrated, regional design/build development companies with offices in twenty-seven locations and more than 1,200 employees from coast to coast. Since its formation, in April 1953, the company—first known as Trojan Construction, then Rauenhorst Construction, then Rauenhorst Corporation, and, finally, Opus—has completed more than 2,100 buildings of all kinds, in small towns, big cities, and suburbs, in virtually every part of the United States. What was originally a one-man general contractorship—with the invaluable help of one good woman—has long since been recognized as an industry giant of unexcelled quality, versatility, and integrity, with in-house capabilities and expertise in real estate development, architecture and engineering, construction, property and asset management, financing, leasing, and sales.

Its projects, more specifically, range from that original $56,000 Lutheran church in Olivia, Minnesota, to a 3.2-million-square-foot Best Buy Corporation campus on the edge of Minneapolis. Once known for its low-profile warehouses and nondescript office buildings in the Twin Cities, Opus can now showcase striking office towers, sprawling corporate headquarters, "big-box" retail centers, and inspiring educational complexes throughout the nation. Many of those buildings have incorporated cutting-edge engineering achievements and innovations, from fire-safety improvements to energy-saving materials and techniques.

Four Campuses

When he was starting out, Gerry articulated something he had known since he was a kid on the farm—to wit, "I like to build buildings." And it is the buildings that provide the most visible, tangible, and, of course, bankable evidence of his company's enterprise during its first fifty years. Indeed, the company can point to literally thousands of buildings of all kinds—from churches to hockey arenas, from office towers to warehouses —as examples of its work.

Perhaps none of those two-thousand-plus projects, however, says as much about the company—and its founder's vision—at the fifty-year mark as the two "campuses" designed and built by Opus during the past decade and the two currently under way. As it happens, though the term *campus* usually connotes an academic setting, only one of the four is part of a university. But, as a corporate spokesperson has pointed out, "a campus is also a purposeful collection of corporate, industrial, or medical buildings...that integrates the people, products, and processes" on which an enterprise depends.

In Omaha, Nebraska, the Opus-designed and -built campus is the corporate headquarters of ConAgra, the nation's second-largest food company. It comprises 600,000 square feet in five buildings on thirty-five acres abutting the Missouri River in an area of downtown Omaha once blighted with abandoned factories, dilapidated railroad facilities, and environmentally compromised wasteland.

Working with both ConAgra executives and city officials—who were eager to reclaim this historic section of their downtown and keep the big food company in the city—Opus worked out deals with some forty separate land owners, took out two-million square feet of derelict buildings, figured a way to protect worthwhile neighborhood buildings, remediated contaminated soils, and reconfigured the land itself, creating, among other amenities, a fifteen-acre lake around which the new corporate buildings would cluster. The buildings themselves were designed, by Opus architect John Albers, in the Prairie School style of Frank Lloyd Wright and linked by bright, art-lined underground passageways for year-round comfort and convenience. The two-and-a-half-year project was opened on September 17, 1990.

"We picked Opus because we believed we'd get the best job at the best price, and we were right," said a satisfied and happy Mike Harper, ConAgra's chairman at the time.

The second of the three is actually the centerpiece of a major university—in this case, the downtown Minneapolis site of the University of St. Thomas, now Minnesota's largest private university. And the inspiration was notably academic.

"One day in 1964," as Gerry likes to tell the story, "Hanky and I were driving through Oxford, England. We stopped at the front entrance of the Christ Church College and walked in. 'Wow!' I thought. 'Wouldn't it be nice to build something like this some day?'"

Not quite forty years later "some day" arrived. Opus had completed twenty projects on two of St. Thomas's campuses (in St. Paul and Owatonna, Minnesota), expanding a distinctive architectural style that was at once classic and contemporary. It was in the late 1980s that UST officials turned to Opus to create a new urban campus that would suggest the stately architectural style of the four-century-old Christ Church campus that had so impressed Gerry and Hanky in the 1960s.

Begun in 1992, with Terrence Murphy Hall, the Minneapolis campus, when its law school facility and Opus-built parking ramp (operated by the city of Minneapolis) were completed in 2003, comprised four structures, designed in the Collegiate Gothic style of its St. Paul counterpart, clad in native Kasota stone, and arranged around an open green quad. Three more buildings are contemplated, including the future home of the St. Thomas School of Entrepreneurship.

Like the ConAgra headquarters in Omaha, the new St. Thomas campus has turned around an unsightly and underutilized part of its historic downtown. "Their charge [was to] design an entire campus that our constituents would recognize and associate architecturally with the quality education which had become a hallmark of our main [St. Paul] campus," said Terrence Murphy, former St. Thomas president and now chancellor. "They did a masterful job."

When the nation's largest consumer-electronics retailer, Best Buy Corporation, decided to consolidate fourteen separate suburban Twin Cities facilities at a single headquarters site, the first question was where. At the request of Best Buy's founder and chairman Richard Schulze, Opus analyzed eight possible venues—with an eye on employee commute time, local traffic flow, vehicle and pedestrian accessibility, city incentives, tax increment financing considerations, building configuration, and visibility. The site finally chosen was the south Minneapolis suburb of Richfield, near the intersection of I-494 and I-35.

There were other requirements, too. The Best Buy campus had to be large enough for 7,500 employees, include facilities for on-site daycare, a wellness center, and a 42,000-square-foot "Leadership Institute" for continuing education, and reflect the fun and flair for which the company was known—all at a "feasible" cost to stockholders.

The result—completed in 2003, scarcely eighteen months after groundbreaking, at an equally remarkable $62 per square foot—is huge and striking. The campus comprises 3.6-million square feet in four major buildings, a two-story "community hub," and a parking structure on forty acres readily accessible from around the south metro. The campus is visibly unmistakable, featuring architectural concrete panels with aluminum framed glazing systems and a distinctive wing wall. The concrete used in its construction would be enough to complete a sidewalk from Minneapolis to Milwaukee!

Appropriately enough, when it was time for Gerry to speak (via satellite hookup) to Opus employees around the country on the occasion of the firm's golden anniversary, he chose, at Dick Schulze's invitation, the brand-new Best Buy headquarters. His thinking was obvious: a landmark occasion celebrated at what had instantly become a local landmark.

Gerry gives much credit for the success of these three campuses—two corporate and one collegiate—to John Albers, the company's chief architect. "All three were built in rundown urban locations, which required considerable negotiations with local governments," Gerry explains. "Each required some governmental assistance to make them economically viable. Because of their location in redeveloped areas, there were many utility and environmental hurdles as well. In each case, Opus had complete responsibility for all aspects of the projects, under John's capable guidance and with the cooperation of all the other disciplines and entities—construction, financial, city negotiators, utility people, and others.

"Over the past twenty-eight years," Gerry continues, "John has been our creative bedrock. He is indeed one of the unsung heroes of this company." Gerry recalls once asking John why, with all his talent and ability, he hadn't gone off on his own and hung out his own shingle. John's answer was swift and sweet: "Because here at Opus I design ten buildings and nine get built. My friends who work at architectural firms design ten buildings and maybe *one* gets built. I relish seeing almost everything I design take shape before my eyes."

Importantly, the process continues. A *fourth* major campus is under way in suburban Milwaukee. In this case, the client is Northwestern Mutual, with whom Rauenhorst/Opus has had a long and productive relationship. Opus's Milwaukee office first found land for a new corporate headquarters, then became development manager (hiring an architect, negotiating municipal processes, etc.), then began managing the new complex's construction. Opus is also doing the "concrete work" and landscaping for the massive project, which was formally announced during the summer of 2002. The campus will be developed in four phases and is designed for eight structures: four office buildings and four parking facilities. Phase I is scheduled to be completed in June 2004.

The Northwestern Mutual campus, according to Les Blum, Opus's head man in Milwaukee, has been "master-planned" for 1.9 million to

2 million square feet, and the four phases will be built out over fifteen to twenty years. The campus, when completed, will include a 40,000-square-foot computer center designed "never to go down," with state-of-the-art security and redundancies of everything.

Good People Well Organized

Now with the second generation of Rauenhorsts in key positions, Opus continues to grow, evolve in shape and function, and take advantage of opportunities as they present themselves. Like its founder, however, its growth, even now, is best described as steady and measured, rather than spectacular. "Opus has never outgrown our ability to handle it," Gerry once noted. "Growth is the result of good operation. If you grow for growth's sake, it's not a good thing. If you grow for a reason, it makes sense."

The regional decentralization that Gerry and his top managers began some twenty years ago has served it well. Formally, in 2003, the Opus Group comprises the Opus Corporation, headed by board chairman Keith Bednarowski and president and CEO Mark Rauenhorst; Opus National, under executive vice president Andy Deckas; and five regional operations: Opus East L.L.C., under president Jim Lee, with offices in Philadelphia and Washington, D.C.; Opus North Corporation, under president Jack Crocker, with offices in Chicago, Columbus, Detroit, Indianapolis, and Milwaukee; Opus Northwest, L.L.C., under president John Solberg, with offices in Denver, Kansas City, Minneapolis, Portland, Seattle, and St. Louis; Opus South Corporation, headed by president Joe Rauenhorst, with offices in Atlanta, Fort Lauderdale, Orlando, Pensacola, and Tampa; and Opus West Corporation, under president Tom Roberts, with offices in Austin, Dallas, Houston, Los Angeles, Orange County, Phoenix, Sacramento, San Francisco, and San Jose.

Recently completed or still-in-progress works, besides the afore-mentioned campuses, include a student union at the College of St. Catherine in St. Paul, a library and athletic center at Marquette University in Milwaukee, a student union at Xavier University in Cincinnati, and student apartments at St. Mary's College in South Bend, as well as several major corporate developments, among them a U.S. Bank operations center in St. Paul, the Discount Tire headquarters in Phoenix, and a three-building campus for Microsoft in Seattle.

In 1998, Opus moved into its seventh and latest corporate head-quarters (the first HQ, remember, was the breezeway Gerry constructed in his Richfield home) in Opus 2, in Minnetonka. The complex, by then nearly thirty years old, had proven itself over and over again to the thousands of people who daily traversed its famous dual-road system and worked among its gently rolling hills.

As it happened, however, after Opus 2 had been open for about twenty years, the city of Minnetonka decided the one-way road network was a problem and wanted to convert to a two-way system. To back up their plans, city engineers surveyed Opus 2's occupants, certain to have support for the change. "I don't know how many people or businesses they ended up polling," Gerry says with a smile, "but I do know that only one respondent indicated he was willing to consider a switch. So [the city] decided to leave it the way it is."

Gerry, in fact, has long insisted (and apparently the Opus 2 community would agree) that the street system is one of the enduring strengths of the complex. "The primary roads last forever," he explains, "because there's no sewer, gas, water, telephone, or electric running underneath them. The biggest cost of any utility, particularly in an undulating landscape, is putting, say, a sewer line through a hill. So the first thing we did at Opus 2 was determine the lowest contour and decide that that's where the sewer line would go. We didn't have to dig sewer lines more than ten or twelve feet deep, so we could use a little back hoe and get the job done fast. We put all the utilities in for a small percentage of the usual cost, and all on the secondary roads, not under the main roads. The main roads go up, over, and around the hills at Opus 2. And almost every lot has access to a main road on one side and a secondary road on the other. All the utilities come in from the back, so if something has to be fixed, or maybe more phone lines have to be added, we can do that without having to dig up the main road."

Gerry remains such an unabashed enthusiast of Opus 2 he said recently, "Even at the age of seventy-five I'd love to build another one."

So why hasn't he? "Because this was a unique piece of property," he says of the Minnetonka site. "In fact, I've never seen one quite like it. It's a big piece, too—500 acres—and we just haven't had the chance to acquire such a big piece of land. Believe me, though, I wouldn't hesitate for a moment to build another one if the opportunity presented itself.

"And I know we could do it even better the second time, what with the experience and know-how we've gained since doing the first!"

"First and Foremost, He's a Profit-Making Guy"

Reviewing the manuscript for this book, Opus chairman Keith Bednarowski pointed out what he felt was a serious omission.

"You've described Gerry as a family man, a philanthropist, and an entrepreneur—but no one has spoken about what is perhaps the principal reason for the financial success of Opus—his instinctive business acumen. He wasn't a finance major in college. He doesn't have an MBA. He doesn't have a psychology degree. But Gerry's instincts combine all of that. His instincts are unlike those of anyone I've ever known."

Bednarowski cited five of Gerry's "instincts" that he feels have made Opus the success it is today.

"First is Gerry's profit mentality. First and foremost, he's a profit-making guy. He instinctively knows how to make money. He's the most creative person I know in that respect. He's often said: 'Keith, we're in business to make money. If we're not making money, we're losing money, and I don't like that at all.'

"His focus on building a highly profitable business is unwavering—and it's intense. I've watched this many, many times: He's presented a set of financial statements, his fingers inevitably go to the bottom line, and then he works back from there. Then he starts to ask questions. Penetrating questions. Amazingly insightful questions. He just won't stand for mediocre financial results. A lot of people know about his philanthropy. They note his mild manner and easy smile. Few realize his intense instincts for making money so that he can use it to make a difference in funding the social causes that he believes in. He's a good businessman first; that allows him to be a good philanthropist.

"Second, Gerry has a phenomenal instinct about interest rates, particularly the timing of rates, that I find hard to explain. And he couples that with a good grasp of taxes. For Opus, which borrows a lot of money and places a lot of mortgages and pays a lot of interest, this ability on the part of its leader has been a big contributor to its success. It's an instinct, I believe, that God has given to him. I've seen him, time and time again, fix a particular interest rate with a tenant. We all thought it was a mistake—Fed rates were predicted to rise. But he'd just smile and then wait for the market to fall, and, sure enough, it would. And Opus consequently made an unexpected profit. Unexpected, that is, to everyone except Gerry. He just seemed to know what was going to happen. Some say he gained this knowledge from having served on the board of the Ninth Federal Reserve District. My take is that perhaps it had to do with his study of economics in college, but it's probably more likely that he had this instinct in him the day he was born.

"Third is his ability to do mental arithmetic. That's the only way I can describe it. He can figure out if a deal makes sense faster than any person I know. Recently, a well-known Twin Cities businessman was trying to sell him on investing in a 'good deal.' This man's people had spent days working up the rationale as to why it was a wise investment. They thought they had an answer for any objection. Gerry got there a half-hour late. He had never heard of the deal before. He came in absolutely cold, listened carefully, thought about it for all of five minutes or so, and said, 'It won't work, and here's why.' Everybody was stunned. He'd done the math in his head, and it turned out he was absolutely right. He'd figured out the pitfalls in five minutes. I've seen that happen over and over again through the years. It has saved us millions of dollars when we've done deals that involve significant risks and require large investments.

"Fourth, he's an instinctively conceptual thinker. Gerry can visualize how a deal should work. Then he's able to articulate it. Some people think engineers have tunnel vision. He doesn't. And he's always thinking ahead. He began thinking—I'll bet twenty-five years ago—about how to structure the family business so that it can survive and successfully pass on after his death. The acquisition of Dyson was a good business move for us, but Gerry also saw in it a way to gain a foothold in the South and structure the business so that he could pass on the entire company to the next two generations. Opus 2 was a concept he had thought through for years until the opportunity came to buy the property. He's thinking all the time. Often, he's called me from home at eight or so in the morning and said, 'Keith, I woke up at four o'clock and had this idea.' Then he'd articulate it clearly. Mike Sullivan, one of our outside directors, recently marveled at Gerry's conceptual ability. Mike said, 'After he's thought out an idea, then and only then he looks to accountants, lawyers, and engineers, not so much for their ideas but rather as a sounding board to confirm his thoughts and to poke holes, if they can, in his concepts.' This ability has led to innumerable successes for Opus over the years.

"And fifth, Gerry has an instinct for patience. He's willing, for example, to sit on a property until it can pay off, or to wait for interest rates to turn in his favor, or to wait for the stock market to turn, or to wait out the construction cycle. In the business we're in, this is a great virtue. Our business is not for impatient people, and Gerry isn't."

Mark Rauenhorst, Opus's CEO, agrees that his father has God given instincts that have contributed greatly to his, and thus Opus's, success. But Mark believes that Gerry has certain acquired abilities, too—such as the learned skill set of a superb professional manager. "This is not something he was born with," Mark says. "It was something he consciously set out to learn. He served on boards of larger and smaller companies. He read the business literature. He went to seminars. He hired experts to mentor him. He learned a lot from Clarence Frame, the CEO of First National Bank in St. Paul, who was Gerry's first outside board member. He learned a lot from other outside board members.

"The structuring of the Opus board is an example. Gerry saw the mistakes made by companies whose boards were essentially the CEO's rubber stamp, and realized that such boards are an exercise in futility. Early on, he recruited strong outsiders who understood the culture of a family business and who at the same time were hardheaded business people with proven judgment. A good example is Susan Marvin, president of Marvin Windows. Gerry asked Susan to join the Opus board in 1998. Marvin Windows is a successful Minnesota-based family business whose leadership, in the person of Susan, is now in its third generation. She thoroughly understands the problems inherent in family businesses, and she fully grasps the opportunities. Susan is a great sounding board for our ideas. She helps keep us on track. We are blessed to have her.

"Gerry made it clear from the start—and I've heard him say it frequently—'I don't want "yes" people on our board.' He made it clear that he was giving the board members—particularly the outsiders— fiduciary responsibility and authority. That's very unusual in a private family business.

"Gerry made certain that at Opus everyone is responsible to someone, particularly at the board level. He likes to paraphrase Harry Truman: 'At Opus the buck stops with the board.' Board members know that; they take the responsibility very seriously. He has insisted that we have specific five-year goals, set by the board, and that structures are in place to carry out these goals.

"Another hallmark of Gerry's management is financial discipline. He realized early on that Opus would always be borrowing a lot of money from a lot of banks and other lending institutions. It's the nature of our business. But he always insists on being able to pay off his banking obligations on a moment's notice. Consequently, over fifty years, this company has never missed paying on time principal and interest to any bank. 'The banks will always be important to us, but I don't want to be beholden to them,' he's often said. 'I want us to run our business, not the banks.'

"That means we've had to maintain a very strong balance sheet. We've had to be disciplined to manage our cash flow. Our reputation with the lending institutions is always at the top of his mind. He will never let us do anything to jeopardize that reputation. And that has stood us in good stead, particularly when our business has had its downturns and we've needed help. Our credit lines are excellent.

"And this internal financial discipline flows to our operating regions. Each is required to form its own relationships with the lending institutions in its region. And each is required to manage these relationships itself. Each regional president is a CEO in his own right, with the responsibility and the authority to borrow the funds he needs to manage his cash flow and to maintain profitability.

"This preoccupation with reputation relates to another aspect of Gerry's philosophy that pervades the company: '*How* we do things is often as important as *what* we do.' That means we must work hard at acting honorably, paying our debts promptly, quickly and cheerfully fixing things that may go wrong with our projects. 'Do it right and people will notice,' Gerry likes to say.

"And then there's Gerry's preoccupation with the need to work together. Opus is constantly dealing with large, complicated projects involving large amounts of money. We must bring in a lot of outside parties, multiple disciplines, project managers, sub-contractors, sometimes consulting architects, and many more. Gerry has stressed over and over that the Opus way is to work together and have respect for one another. Big egos don't make it at Opus. They suppress the working-together-with-respect culture. Gerry believes that employees should get to know the people they work with—get to know their families, hobbies, and home life. That helps to establish a culture of rapport and mutual respect."

Regional Perspectives

On the company's fiftieth anniversary, Opus's regional presidents were asked to discuss their respective capabilities, opportunities, and challenges.

Jim Lee, of Opus East, said, "In 1994, it became apparent that suburban Washington, D.C., was a natural fit for Opus. It has since proven to be an excellent platform for Opus's entry into the Northeast."

As Lee points out, however, there have been hurdles for the office. "Opus was virtually unknown within the region. Our national relationships with CB

Richard Ellis, Insignia, Cushman and Wakefield, Bank of America, PNC, and Mellon helped open doors, but we had to deliver successful projects to establish our credibility in the region. We gained our foothold with a successful joint venture with Marriott on a large assisted-living complex. That was immediately followed by two large retail centers.

"We are still the new kid on the block in this area, but people are recognizing that we may actually have a better way of delivering projects. Our integrity and ethical approach is winning us the support and respect of key subcontractors and brokers as we aggressively pursue speculative and design-build opportunities.

"We have established a presence in Washington and Philadelphia, and will be in Boston within a year. Our short-term goal is to become one of the largest warehouse developers in the Northeast while we continue to expand our office and retail development base. We're carefully analyzing the residential multifamily market, and we'll enter that market when the right opportunity presents itself.

"Real estate is a local business, and local market knowledge is a key to our success. Decentralized management keeps the decision process close to the realities and opportunities of the local markets. Our advantages competing at the local level are, one, a strong capital base; two, a national perspective on industry trends; and, three, the cumulative base of knowledge gained from the quantity of projects completed throughout the group.

"We think globally and act locally."

Jack Crocker described Opus North as an "industry-leading real estate and design-build organization" operating in Illinois, Wisconsin, Ohio, Indiana, Michigan, and Kentucky. "Opus North," he said, "is a client-driven creator of space. Using a vertically integrated design-build approach, we develop and redevelop real estate in response to ever-changing user needs and market conditions. Opus North is guided by sound financial principles and an ethical approach to business. It believes it has a responsibility to charitably contribute to the communities in which it operates.

"None of Opus North's markets is considered a 'growth' market. Because of that, we are willing to do complicated redevelopments, even on environmentally challenged properties. By the way, it feels good to take a derelict property and make it productive again while bringing jobs and tax base to an area that typically needs them—all the while making an appropriate profit.

"Opus's core competencies are design, construction, and development —each of which is dramatically influenced by local conditions. As such, a fundamentally decentralized system is the only effective operating model. Each regional company responds to opportunities with local deal-making authority that is supported by an organization of unparalleled depth and breadth of expertise and a strong capital base."

Opus Northwest's John Solberg addressed Opus's success not just during the past fifty years but looking ahead to the next fifty years as well.

According to Solberg, Opus has been, and will continue to be, successful because:

"Opus understands the business it's in and is willing to take the risks necessary to be successful on a large scale. So many companies you see in our industry are either not prepared to take the kind of risks we need to take or assume bad risks and go out of business.

"Opus is ethical and, as such, attracts the kind of employees and customers that give a company longevity.

"Opus has effectively decentralized. Real estate is a local business, and people do business with people they know and trust.

"Opus knows how to delegate, in our founder's words, 'large and equal amounts of responsibility and authority.'

"Opus has developed an excellent design/build framework. I've worked for pure construction companies and pure developers, and have the perspective of seeing the benefit of Opus's design/build system. That system gives the customer better value and allows Opus to reduce its risks."

Opus West was founded in 1980 to focus primarily on the office development market, says its president, Tom Roberts. After a sharp drop in business and resulting staff cuts in 1990, the company has bounced back dramatically, thanks in large part to geographic and product diversification.

More specifically, Roberts says, "with the office development market flat on its back in the West, Opus moved aggressively into retail development, a segment that was new to the region but was growing, especially in the still-robust Phoenix market." The company worked hard to develop a quality image, particularly for developing open-air shopping centers that mix retail, dining, and entertaining. "Between 1993 and 1996, more than seventy-five percent of the region's business was in retail," Robert explains. "Then, when the office market began coming back in the mid-1990s, we had the skilled professionals in place and we were able to grow steadily. During this time frame, Opus West opened regional offices in northern and southern California." In 2002, the region was expanded to include Texas when Opus West took over Opus South's assets in that market.

"From 1996 through 2002, the West region was able to develop millions of square feet of office, industrial, and retail space," Roberts continues. "Opus West had become the dominant player in the western United States. In Phoenix, it's been named Developer of the Year nine times in the past eleven years."

In 2002, as the office market softened again, the regional business again began to change its focus, developing multifamily housing—apartment buildings—especially in northern California and Texas, with more than a thousand units under way in 2003 and a realistic expectation of two thousand units by 2004. (Opus West remains active in industrial and retail development.)

Roberts attributes the region's success to a strategy that directs responsibility down from regional headquarters to the individual office level. "The local offices," he says, "are near their customers and know what's going on. They can move quickly and decisively." Managers in those offices "have responsibility and authority, which they thrive on, and they're handsomely rewarded if they're successful." It's all part of Opus's entrepreneurial culture that permeates the organization from top to bottom.

Joe Rauenhorst heads Opus South, which originated with the acquisition of Dyson & Company, of Pensacola, Florida, twenty years ago. "Dyson gave Opus an important base in the southeast," Joe says. "It brought a southeastern presence and a reputation for integrity, and Opus was quickly able to bring its vertically integrated design-build approach to the business."

While continuing to maintain a construction office in Pensacola, Opus moved the regional headquarters to Tampa and swiftly branched into real estate development to capitalize on the office and the residential boom in the region at the time. Joe took over Opus South in 2002, filling the vacancy created when his brother Neil left to start his own business. "I was fortunate," Joe says, "because Neil left behind a superb reputation for quality and integrity.

"When customers know you, when you're respected, when they associate you with values and integrity, you have a distinct advantage when you're competing for business," he continues. "When I moved to Opus South, I experienced first-hand how vital a reputation is and how important it is to guard it.

"Using the Dyson base, Opus South was able to grow over the ensuing twenty years into a full-fledged, diversified real estate development company, expanding into Orlando, Fort Lauderdale, and Atlanta. By the end of 2002, the Opus South region had an annual volume in excess of $200 million and employed about sixty people. It was building mixed use retail and residential projects throughout the Southeast and important industrial projects in Tennessee, Florida, Texas, and Georgia."

Joe says one of the strengths of Opus South is its ability to be successful in many product types. "We're consistently competitive when bidding on office, residential, industrial, retail, and mixed use office building projects," he explains. "But our involvement in each of these segments, as a percentage of our entire business at Opus South, changes, sometimes quickly, depending on which market is strongest. Versatility is one of our greatest assets.

"Right now [in 2003], office construction is generally slow in the Southeast, but retail and residential activity is strong, so we've been able to quickly shift our main focus into that area, where we'll continue to focus until the office building and industrial markets come back. Opus South has become particularly experienced and very versatile—nimble—moving with the cycles. For example, Florida is, and will be for a long time to come, a strong residential and mixed retail market for us. Some 300,000 people move into the state every year, and they all need a place to live and shop. So we're very busy building condominiums and shopping centers. We have developed fifteen Publix grocery stores that anchor retail centers. And we're very excited about the opportunities to build mixed-use condominiums.

"We're concentrating our condominium efforts exclusively on waterfront locations. Waterfront is in great demand in Florida. People who move here tend to do so because they want to be on the water. And our office building projects in Florida all have a mixed-use element—that is, an office building with a retail component as part of it. That's working very well.

"But I can't stress enough the flexibility we have at the region level—we're able to move very fast when we see changes in the marketplace. We don't have to go through a bunch of meetings at headquarters. We don't have to sit around and wait for a lot of approvals. That's what's great about the Opus philosophy that Gerry laid down years ago. We know that we in each region are responsible for our success—and our failure. We know that authority to make most decisions is clearly delegated to each region. So when we see an opportunity, a change in the cycle, we can move quickly."

After summarizing the several strengths of Opus South—its long time in the market ("We're well-known"), its reputation for integrity ("We tell the truth"), the quality of its work ("We build good buildings"), Joe adds, "But perhaps our greatest strength is that our company's best salesman lives only ninety miles from our regional headquarters. When we need him, Gerry is only an hour and a half away.

"Recently, Gerry came with me to St. Petersburg, where we'd been having trouble acquiring a piece of land from a dentist who was in his late seventies or early eighties. Dad, who's seventy-five years old himself, told the dentist about Opus and how he got started, about how we do business, and about the era they both grew up in. It was all very low-key and no pressure, and that made the man comfortable. Soon after, we completed the purchase."

On a more personal level, Joe, who had a successful eight-year career as a litigator in a leading law firm and became partner before joining Opus, says he prefers what he's doing right now. "The law is one of the most costly and inefficient ways in the world to resolve disputes, but that's what it's all about," he explains. "For me, it's a heck of a lot more rewarding to be in a productive business where, at the end of the day, you've created something important—jobs, places for people to live and work, a better environment. So I'm very happy where I am. I don't even mind, though I grew up in the North, Florida's summer temperatures. I just jump in the pool a lot more often."

Encore One

"About three and a half years ago," Gerry says, "we held a two-day session to discuss a five-year plan. The big question was, Where will we be *twenty-five* years from now? We used growth components about half of what we'd had in the past. Yet it was amazing what our growth projections for the next twenty-five years showed. We were reminded, to say the least, what a large company Opus has become, and that if it continues to be half as successful as it's been up to now, it will become a very large company indeed.

"At the same meeting, we discussed whether all of our eggs should be in one basket. My normal reply to that question is, 'I don't mind if they're all in one basket as long as we watch that basket.' Still, at some point it makes sense to have some diversification. Our biggest challenge is that we are in a very volatile cycle, businesswise. Right now, in late 2003, we will probably start only one or two office buildings while normally we'd have twenty-five or thirty in the works. That's a pretty dramatic swing. Instead, we've been getting extensively into residential work—condos and apartments. In another year or two, about half of our business may be residential, though, if office buildings get hot again, we'll be back at them very quickly.

"Anyway, at that long-range planning session, we decided to find businesses *not* subject to the same cycles Opus is. So we started a side company, independent of Opus, called Encore One, run by Keith Bednarowski. The purpose of Encore One is to look for and acquire other businesses. The criteria would include a flatter business cycle, significant synergies with Opus, and excellent existing management (because we don't want to manage the acquired company). The acquired company's owner, for that matter, would ideally be a lot like me—except that he or she wouldn't have any children ready and able to take over the business.

"Encore One's first major acquisition—a Minneapolis-based company named Marsden—was completed in 2002. The owner, who is about my age, wanted to sell to someone who would take care of his employees, preserve the name of the company, and keep it profitably in business. It's actually in three different businesses. One is cleaning buildings. Obviously, right there the synergy is great: We have buildings that need to be cleaned. What's more, they want to expand to Phoenix. Well, we have buildings in Phoenix that need cleaning, so, in due course, they will have a branch in Phoenix. Their second business is security—which means more synergy, because we need security in our buildings. Their third business is money transfer. They own between 125 and 150 armored cars, and transfer money for ATMs and so forth. There's not much synergy for Opus in that one, but money transfer is a growth business. In fact, all three of these businesses can grow even in slow economic times. Meanwhile, Marsden employs a total of about 6,000 people. Most of them are cleaning people, and many are Somalis and Hmong, who the company want to learn English and for whom the company provides instruction, thus offering a very real benefit to the community, too.

"All told, we probably looked at a hundred companies before we found one that fit. Now, at this point, we're probably through the next hundred. We'll keep looking, and when we find others that offer the same kind of pluses that Marsden does, we'll buy it."

A Finger on the Pulse

The single obvious constant from one end of Opus's fifty-year continuum to the other is, of course, the founding chairman himself. Gerry will be the first to tell you he has learned a great deal over the years and certainly has adapted to the many changes great and small that have affected his corporate and business lives. But those closest to him insist that he's basically the same guy he's always been.

Mike Sullivan, an Opus board member since 1994, remarks on Gerry's consistency. "He doesn't change," Sullivan says. "He's always been a long-range thinker—and I mean long, *long* range. He's always known what he wants to accomplish, and how to make people buy into it."

Luz Campa, who has been Gerry's chief tax advisor since joining the company in 1974, says, "Gerry is a driven man. He's driven to do things right. He's a very smart businessman. Not only that, but he loves business. He loves what he does. Every aspect of it. Another secret to his success is that he surrounds himself with smart people. Then he encourages these smart people to hire additional smart people. Then he makes sure all those smart people are rewarded handsomely when they succeed."

Campa describes, for example, the incentive and compensation plan he helped Gerry, Mark, and Keith Bednarowski devise for the company's top managers. Previously, the managers were given stock in the company. More recently, they have been enrolled in a "phantom stock plan" that, according to Campa, provides them with "virtually the same economic benefits as real ownership without the hassle." He says, "Equity complicates one's life with all the record-keeping and follow-up that's involved. The phantom stock plan that Opus has devised provides an incentive to the manager without being burdensome.

"Very simply, a phantom loan is made to the manager to enable that person to acquire a given number of phantom shares. The phantom shares have a value equal to the book value of an equivalent number of shares of common stock in the company. The loan gets paid off out of the dividends that are generated if the region is successful. Once the loan is paid off, the dividends from the phantom stock are paid to the individual.

The manager's interests are therefore aligned with the same interests that an owner would have.

"It's all very bottom line. The plan aligns all the interests of the parties with each other." Campa adds that several managers have told him how much they appreciated and were motivated by the program.

Campa, officially Opus's senior vice president in charge of tax matters, has actually known Gerry since Campa was a young accountant at Arthur Andersen and Campa's first client was Rauenhorst Construction. Campa points out that Gerry was keenly interested in tax matters from the beginning. Campa, for his part, remembers being impressed that, "as a businessman, Gerry instinctively understood that income taxes can take a huge bite out of net earnings and that a good project can be made better by good tax planning."

When Campa joined Rauenhorst in 1974, he reported to Bob Perkins, who was then the company's chief financial officer, and was responsible for tax planning and making sure tax returns were filed in a timely manner. "As the business grew and real estate transactions continued to lend themselves to creative tax planning," he says, "Gerry and I began working together more closely." To this day, though Gerry is no longer part of day-to-day management, the two men continue to meet and "toss around ideas," often over lunch.

According to Campa, Gerry believes the government should get every dollar it's entitled to under the law, but to pay more by failing to utilize all appropriate provisions legally granted a business is to deprive that business of money that can be used to grow. Campa thus operates by a very specific rule: "Work out Gerry's taxes so he pays the correct amount, but not one penny more."

Lately, Campa, as well as other colleagues, have remarked on Gerry's uncanny knack for staying on top of things, even after his so-called retirement.

"He has an innate ability, even though he's not present in the office, and even after retiring, to keep his finger on the pulse of the place," Campa says. Gerry can be away from headquarters for weeks at a time, but when he returns, he knows exactly what's going on. What's more, says Campa, "he has a legendary memory and the ability to ask the right questions."

Tom Roberts, president of Opus West, says he, too, has been amazed by how closely the founder is attuned to the workings of the company, even when his attention is focused on outside interests.

"He always seems to know exactly what is happening," Roberts says. "His ability to keep in touch is phenomenal. Frankly, I don't know how he does it."

Roberts laughs, then adds, "It's kind of an eerie feeling, but I think Gerry will somehow have his finger on the pulse of this place forever. Even when he's gone, I think we'll be feeling his presence."

Chapter Seven

Legacy

"Dad left the farm, got a good education, started his own business, and was very successful. And he's been able to help a lot of other folks along the way...."

Such, in a nutshell, is Gerry Rauenhorst's extraordinary life and career, as neatly described by son Neil.

Who could argue? But let's not leave it at that.

Impact and Influence

Recently, *Twin Cities Business Monthly* noted:

When considering whether Gerald Rauenhorst has had an impact on construction and development in the United States, first consider the more than 2,000 buildings Opus has constructed around the country. Then take stock of the fact that Opus revolutionized the building industry by being one of the first firms to unite the disparate worlds of architecture and construction into a team. And don't forget that the National Association of Industrial and Office Properties named Opus the National Developer of the Year in 1992....

Over the years, Opus has changed the face of the Twin Cities with the many projects it has developed and built, including the fifty-three-story U.S. Bancorp building and the American Express Financial Advisors skyscraper in downtown Minneapolis....

The company's legacy, as the *Business Monthly* tribute suggests, includes more than buildings and corporate offices. Gerry was indeed a pioneer of the design/build approach; he decided that the historic tension between architects and contractors was a wasteful and inefficient tradition, and that horizontally integrating the two functions was a much better way of getting the job done right. Beginning in the early 1960s, he combined design and build functions in a turnkey approach and accepted responsibility for every step of the building process. Derided by architects and other builders, and resisted by clients, the design/build concept was eventually accepted and widely adopted. But Rauenhorst/Opus had a leg up on the competition and solidified its reputation with excellent work finished on time and within budget.

Of course, Gerry would say that design/build was but another manifestation of the kind of professional and personal integrity that he found wanting in the construction industry when he started in 1953. It was, to be sure, a superior way of getting a project built, but, more important, it represented a mindset that placed a premium on value and integrity from start to finish. "Success," Gerry remarked in *Real Estate Forum* a few years ago, "is based on nothing really startling or spectacular. Essentially, it's being honest with people. Trends and technologies come and go, but that one thing will never change."

The company's clients have agreed. Mike Harper, who was ConAgra's chairman and CEO when Opus designed and built the big food company's corporate campus in Omaha in the late 1980s and early 1990s, offered the following observation:

> You really don't hire Opus or any of its competitors—you hire the individuals who are going to do the job for you. You can look at the pictures of the jobs they built, you can talk to people who have been clients to see if they're satisfied, but you're really trying to decide who are the best *people* to do the job. Anybody can hire a bulldozer or a crane, anybody can get into the construction business. But it's the quality of the individuals that make great [construction] companies.

And it starts at the top. In Opus's case, it starts with Gerry, a real class act. He's quiet but a very good thinker, and honest as the day is long.

John Nasseff, who was vice president for facilities and engineering at Twin Cities-based West Publishing Company when Opus built several corporate buildings for the firm, had this to say about the process and relationship in a 1994 interview:

> Everything that's there, Opus built. I tell my friends, "I don't take bids on jobs. I deal with people." I don't deal with numbers. Figures lie, and liars figure. If you put something out on bid and you have your plans and specifications, there are many ways you can cut corners. So I don't take bids anymore.
>
> If I were to take a bid today on any building that we want to build, I will guarantee you Rauenhorst would not be the lowest. They'll be in the middle or they'll be higher. But on completion of the job, when it's ready for occupancy, I'll guarantee you our move-in cost per square footage will be cheaper because of the quality that we insist on. Our buildings are quality, first class. That's where a lot of the money goes.
>
> There are several words [that apply]: honesty, sincerity, accommodating. If you look up those words, you'll find a picture of Gerry Rauenhorst. He's very honest, and his company does quality work.

Nasseff would recall a particular incident following the construction of West's facilities. One day he noticed a dip where the blacktop had settled outside one of the new buildings. He called Vic Buchholz, Opus's general superintendent, and told him about the irregularity. A few weeks later, Nasseff happened to think about the blacktop, called Buchholz, and asked when Opus was going to correct the problem.

Buchholz said, "Go look out the window."

Which Nasseff did. "Hey, it's fixed!" he said, surprised and delighted, when he returned to the phone.

"That building was built on an old junkpile," Gerry says. "It was too small a job to do soil tests, so we just put in the blacktop where they told us to. Afterward, we could have argued forever about who was responsible [for the flaw] and therefore liable to pay for the repair. But that's not the way we do business. If we have a problem, rather than argue about who's right or wrong, we prefer to go in and take care of it. Often, determining who's right or wrong is difficult, time-consuming, and expensive. Rather than bringing in the lawyers, we've always preferred to say, 'To heck with it,' and then go fix the problem ourselves.

"As for John and West Publishing—well, from that day forward they never used another contractor."

"I remember when I first went to Chicago," Joe Rauenhorst, offering a somewhat different perspective, yet much the same conclusion, recalled a few years ago, "I met a few former Opus employees, who said they really respected the company because of the values the company stood for, and that they really appreciated working in a place that had the honesty and integrity that Opus had. These were a couple of people I met at various functions, and out of the blue they just told me that. They had never experienced working somewhere that had the integrity that Opus had. That stuck with me."

Those impressions, for that matter, haven't changed during the generational transition, which is testimony to both generations—and to the men and women they've gathered around them. As Mark Rauenhorst has pointed out about the ongoing effort:

> It takes work to continue to do the right thing when it comes to running an enterprise and preserving the good things. It isn't without its challenges, but so far I think we can be very proud of the job we're doing. One of the things we've tried to focus on is to continue to adapt to the change. We're all individuals changing and growing. The key is to adapt to the change while preserving our basic values and principles.

To me, the most important thing in our long-term effectiveness as a business is to continue to hold on to those founding values and principles. As people change, we try to answer the question of what binds us together, how we are similar, as well as how we are different. There is still a lot that binds us, and a lot of that is our shared belief in those basic values and beliefs.

As described in Chapter Four, through innovative programs like 1/40 and Progress Valley, as well as its sustained generosity through Catholic Charities, Habitat for Humanity, the United Way, and other outside philanthropic organizations, Rauenhorst/Opus has long enjoyed a reputation for giving and personal involvement in its various communities. That is also an ongoing part of the company's legacy.

Director, Friend, Teacher

Gerry set a standard, too, with his personal involvements with other outstanding companies, institutions, and causes, both at home and in locations where Opus does business. He became an essential member of several prestigious boards, where his steady, easygoing, but acutely focused presence and counsel would be highly valued.

"I knew when Gerry joined the ConAgra board [in 1982] that we were getting a good man," says Mike Harper. "I didn't know at the time we were getting a damn good *director* as well. But that's what I learned in a hurry and what I came to appreciate about him so much—that he had very good judgement, that he thought things through, and that he could so effectively communicate his thoughts to his fellow directors and to management. He was always very soft-spoken, but when he spoke, people knew they should listen."

St. Thomas president Dennis Dease speaks to Gerry's longtime (indeed record-setting) performance on the university's board of trustees:

He's been very influential, but not with dramatic speeches or interventions at board meetings. When key decisions have to be

205

made, he prefers to meet quietly with individual trustees, other decision-makers, on the golf course or over lunch or during a walk on the beach or in other informal venues in the months before the decision is brought to a vote. He's very effective on that level. That's how the consensus was created, for example, that made it possible for us to move forward with the law school.

The other trustees just trust him. They know he has good judgment and that he knows and cares about the institution so much.

I've served on that board for more than twenty years, and I have never seen him throw his weight around at meetings. He's usually very quiet. And then when he does make a comment, he does it with a certain modesty and obviously with a lot of thought. As the old television commercial goes, "When Gerry speaks, people listen."

"When people speak about the success of the University of St. Thomas, it's quite common to mention the name of Gerald Rauenhorst in the same breath," Eugene Frey, a Minneapolis businessman and UST trustee, has pointed out. "The university has had a distinguished group of trustees over the years, but no one person stands above Gerry Rauenhorst, both for his very generous giving and for his vision and leadership. And, incidentally, most of his giving has been anonymous."

"In my mind," Leo Reding says, "having known him since 1945, when we were roommates at St. Thomas, the one thing that has always stood out about Gerry has been his ability to utilize the talents of the people around him and in turn to give of himself to assist and help other people. I have always felt that this ability was the reason for his great success in the private sector and has been the main reason he has been able to serve so effectively as a university trustee."

"Gerry is known throughout the United States as a man who constructs buildings," according to Robert Wild, S.J., president of Marquette University. "However, at Marquette, he is better described as a creator and builder of a better future for generations of our students."

After earning his degree and teaching at Marquette, Father Wild continued, he was active in alumni affairs even during his early years building his business.

It was therefore natural that when this university decided in 1969 to replace its small all-Jesuit Board of Trustees with a much larger board whose membership would be made up of mostly lay men and women that it would soon turn to Gerry as one of its most successful and consistently dedicated alumni to ask him to join this restructured board.

From 1970 to 2000, he was a member of that body, serving for many of those years as a member of the board's Executive Committee and from 1985 to 1987 as board chair. Indeed, no one has ever held board membership at Marquette for more years than Gerry Rauenhorst. When he stepped down, his fellow board members, as a sign of their profound respect for all that he had done for this university, elected him a trustee emeritus and empowered me as president to confer upon him an honorary degree at our 2001 commencement exercises. Rarely do we award honorary degrees for this sort of thing, but in Gerry's case, given his imaginative and committed leadership on our board and his creative leadership in the field of commercial construction, it seemed an entirely appropriate thing to do. I would add that both in his formal role as board member and otherwise, he has been a wise counselor and good friend to three Marquette presidents, myself included....

Gerry's presence and leadership were always beneficial in the deliberations of our Board of Trustees.... He has a quiet yet definite way of providing leadership and of being the voice of reason, particularly when a fellow member is proposing or encouraging a course of action that would tend to steer the university away from its core mission. All of this Gerry does because he truly cares for young people and wants to help develop graduates who will be transformed at all levels by their education and empowered to be a leaven for good in our society.

Despite his relatively low profile in the larger community, Gerry's championing of private education in general and his alma maters in particular has often become part of the public discussion that characterizes a healthy democracy. In the early eighties, for instance, the Minneapolis *Star Tribune* reported, on its op-ed pages, Gerry's call for a great private university with engineering and other high-technology programs based in the Twin Cities. He made the suggestion to then-Minnesota Governor Rudy Perpich and articulated it further in an Opus newsletter item that garnered considerable attention.

As Leonard Inskip, the *Star Tribune's* associate editor at the time, remarked, "From that modest beginning, Rauenhorst's proposal has rippled the educational pond in widening circles. The Minnesota High Technology Council is interested. Corporate executives have discussed it. The College of St. Thomas...is considering it.

"A strong believer in free-market competition," Inskip continued, "Rauenhorst argues that competition in engineering education could help the [University of Minnesota]. When St. Thomas added a master's degree program in business administration in the 1970s, the [public] university beefed up its program in response. Now, the [University of Minnesota's] business program, Rauenhorst said, is in 'far better shape than it was ten years ago.'"

A few years later, the College of St. Thomas began offering master's degrees in software engineering and manufacturing. Today, the software program is the largest of its kind in the world, and the engineering program is enormously popular with students and local industry alike. And, of course, in 1991, St. Thomas became a university in its own right.

And, about the same time during the early eighties that he was attracting attention for those initiatives, Gerry was turning heads with his outspoken advocacy of the deregulation of education across America. Writing in *Catholics Today* magazine in 1983, he said in part:

> There is one public service provided to U.S. citizens in which the recipient has no choice of provider. A citizen who receives

Medicare has the right to select his hospital and doctor. A food-stamp recipient may select his own grocery store. Welfare payments and unemployment benefits are provided in dollars: the recipient chooses where to spend them. In one most important service, however, there is no choice whatsoever—education....

I suggest that the time is right for deregulation of education. In this age of concern for the consumer, our government has seen fit to deregulate the telephone company and the airlines, and is working on the banks.... It's my contention that until such time as the educational system is [similarly] deregulated and the consumer is allowed an element of choice in schools and in teachers, we will see little, if any, improvement [in public education]....

I believe it's time for every citizen to take an active part in correcting the system. I suggest that we begin by promoting competition, rewarding superior performance, and eliminating seniority as the sole criterion for teacher retention....

Gerry's opinion piece was noticed in, among other places, the United States Senate, where then U.S. Senator David Durenberger read it, in its entirety, into the *Congressional Record*. And, though many of the problems of the public school system remain twenty years later, some of the steps Gerry advocated—including the use of vouchers and teacher-performance incentive plans—have been implemented in many districts across the country.

Then there's the legacy of Gerry as cherished personal friend. Many (though not all) of Gerry's closest relationships have come, reasonably enough, through business and related activities, but the respect and affection have grown far beyond business matters.

Mike Harper is an example at hand. "I just liked him from the beginning," Harper, who lives in Omaha, says of his pal. "He never puts on airs—what you see is what you get. He's just a great guy in every respect. The only problem is, now that we're both so-called retired, I don't see as much of him as I'd like."

Ned Bechtold, the CEO of Payne and Dolan, in Waukesha, Wisconsin, says: "We come from different religious backgrounds, but that's just one of the things that make our relationship interesting. I'm Lutheran and went to public school, so we have a lot of fun talking about our differences. I like to remind him that his first job was building that Lutheran church in Olivia. He says he helped the ecumenical movement by building that church!

"Gerry's the kind of guy who always looks at the plus side of things. He doesn't look at the negatives, at the differences. As far as religion is concerned, he'd rather look at the things we have in common than at the things that separate us, and he'd point out that what we have in common is about ninety-eight percent of the whole."

Bechtold, who's nine years younger than Gerry and typical of the close friends Gerry has developed over the years with diverse individuals in diverse settings, adds, "He's the big brother I never had."

Gene Frey, former CEO of the Waldorf Corporation and a colleague on the St. Thomas Board of Trustees, has known Gerry since 1987. Frey says:

"He always speaks in measured tones. You won't see him get worked up and excited and pound on the table. If he feels strongly about something—and on most subjects he's not lukewarm—he will let people know and people will listen to him. I think when people know that Gerry feels a particular way about something, they don't easily disagree, though he's never pushy.

"He's a man of strong loyalties: to his church, his family, his friends, his business. I'd call him a traditionalist—very conservative in his dress, his politics, his spending. He usually flies commercial class, and there's never been a corporate jet.

"He's a genuinely modest guy, yet he's justifiably proud of his accomplishments, and of doing things his way. He's proved that a person can be successful *and* honest."

And Paul Webber, a retired manufacturer's representative who met Gerry at a Serra Club meeting more than thirty years ago, provides yet another perspective:

"Our friendship has had nothing to do with business.

"We've fished together and played golf together, and we've gotten together with our families in our homes. Once we took a river-barge trip in southern France, another time on the Shannon River in Ireland. It was interesting to see a man who's so obviously dedicated to his business— and who's been so successful at it—able to divorce himself from it when he's away. He's a man with a lot of interests, and he's able to speak on a lot of different subjects, including some subjects that might surprise you. He'll talk at length about ceramics, for instance, because making pottery in his basement is one of his hobbies. A lot of people don't know that.

"It was always obvious that this is a man who knows how to handle success. He is a truly balanced man."

Gerry, though primarily a builder of buildings and corporations, has played a role as a teacher as well—first, in the engineering department at Marquette while still a student himself, then, in later years, as an occasional adjunct professor and guest lecturer at St. Thomas and the University of Minnesota. His commitment to education of all kinds and at all levels is, of course, part of the legacy he received from his parents, especially his mother. On his own, and most recently, he's been particularly interested in teaching both the basics and the fine points of principled entrepreneurship.

"People debate whether an entrepreneur is born or made," he says. "In my opinion, the answer is, 'Both.' Some people could never be an entrepreneur because they lack the basic qualities. You could give them the best formal education in the world and train them for twenty years, and they still wouldn't get there. Other people—like Dick Schulze, who never went to college but who started Best Buy and is now one of the most respected businessmen in Minnesota—just have it in them, and with some training and improvement, they make it.

"People say you can't teach entrepreneurship, and they may be right. I do believe, however, based on my own experience, that your upbringing and the environment in which you're brought up has a huge effect. All of my brothers were entrepreneurs. That's just the way they were. So, for that matter, were my parents, though you don't usually think of farmers as entrepreneurs. With them, it was as much a state of mind as anything—and the way they encouraged their children to look at opportunity.

"I remember an old man saying about my father, 'He's going to be either the richest man in town or the poorest!' Well, my dad went bankrupt, but that doesn't mean he didn't go for the prize. Nothing ventured, nothing gained. That's what an entrepreneur understands, whether he's had a formal education or not.

"But you can help individuals figure out if they're entrepreneurial material, and then give them the education to help them get there sooner than if they just learned it out in the field the way I did. That's what the entrepreneurship program at St. Thomas is about: helping potential entrepreneurs get there sooner."

And friends and colleagues are quick to point out the presence and contributions of Hanky Rauenhorst, who has long been a valued member of the family's various communities as well.

Sister Andrea Lee, president of the College of St. Catherine, gratefully notes, for instance, Hanky's gifts to *her* alma mater, where she served on the school's board of trustees for nine years during the eighties. From 1989 to 1994, she was honorary chair of St. Catherine's capital campaign.

"We all feel she epitomizes the image of a St. Catherine graduate," Sister Andrea explains. "Anyone who has known her over the years can feel her inner strength and resolve, her talent, her graciousness, her values, her social skills, her faith, her appreciation of music and art. And she's the first to say that her years here have helped shape these qualities.

"Personally, I'm grateful to have her for a friend and a colleague. And what an asset she's been to Mr. Rauenhorst."

The Family Business

The legacy that Gerry has been most concerned about, however, is that of the family business—his own, of course, for his own reasons, but also the family business in general, as a vital component of a healthy, prosperous, capitalistic society.

It's hardly a recent preoccupation.

One way or another, in fact, Gerry has been acutely aware of business as a family enterprise—and, therefore, an inextricable part of the life of the family itself—since before he could put the idea in words. It was, after all, the family business he was engaged in that dismal March day more than seventy years ago when he trudged through the mud with his parents and siblings from one tenant farm to another. It was the family business he was contributing to when he and his brothers raised turkeys and shucked corn and constructed that little baseball park in Olivia. It was most definitely a family business he started in 1953, even though the family—he and Hanky—was just large enough to qualify for the designation. Needless to say, during the subsequent raising of their own large brood beginning shortly after the company's founding, the concerns of the business and the family have been tightly entwined.

In a 1994 interview, Gerry revealed both the depth and breadth of those concerns. Asked about the company's transition from his and Hanky's generation to that of their children (and, presumably, to their children's children), he said:

> Hanky wonders on occasion, as I do, whether it's always the best thing, but really it is. I have often said it's very difficult to raise a family, very difficult to run a private business, and it's geometrically more difficult to run a family business—but geometrically more rewarding, too. So if you can do it, you should.
>
> At the moment, we're still plugging along, and I think we have a good chance of surviving for a while. I don't know what will happen when I'm gone; that will be up to somebody else. But what I really like to feel is that we're designing a system that will work if [future generations of the family] want to carry on. A lot of things get going. The culture gets built in, and, if you get it headed in the right direction, things tend to keep going that way....
>
> Unfortunately, the United States is unique in its lack of respect for family businesses. We tend to tax them out of existence, tend

to make sure they don't succeed from generation to generation, with 50 percent tax on each generation. The Asians and Europeans are different. They encourage and reward family businesses. In Germany, we have friends who are in the *seventh* generation of a family business—240 descendents, through two world wars, still doing fine. A few years ago, when I spent some time with people in the Rockefeller office in New York, I learned that John D. Rockefeller decided that America should be different. At the age of fifty-five, he walked out of Standard Oil and never set foot back in the office and forbade his descendents to work there. He divided the company up and gave it to his children. That created a lot of public companies in America and generated taxation that favored public companies over family companies, and made it difficult for a family business to go from one generation to the next. You don't see many family businesses surviving from generation to generation in America.

This is something I've been working on. Back in 1982, following the example of certain European companies that survived from generation to generation, we formed two family trusts. The trusts are designed to last from one generation of beneficiaries to the next generation, in perpetuity. The trusts purchased the Dyson Construction Company. This company continued to grow and is known today as the Opus Group of Companies.

In the same conversation, Gerry was asked what he and Hanky have done to prepare their children for eventual company ownership. Gerry replied:

The business has been deeply ingrained in the family. If somebody asked the kids where they learned about the business, they'd say at the dinner table at night. We all talked about what we did during the day. I would say I got this job today or that job. Then all four boys worked in heavy, dirty construction when they were young. All the kids worked in the office at least one summer, just to see what the office was like. Later, we put a great emphasis on education. All of the kids have at least one advanced degree.

We started having family meetings [in about 1984]. At that time, the only thing we could find [in the way of formal family business education] was at the Wharton School in Philadelphia. So everybody in the family took at least one seminar there. Then we engaged Peter Davis from Wharton to come to our family meetings. We've also had different facilitators. Now we're meeting for a couple days twice a year. Gradually, business matters have started to demand more time [at the meetings]. Where once it was mostly family relations, now it's more issues involving business. Until recently, I sort of "mother-henned" the situation. As the kids have gotten more involved, they've taken more responsibility. We're working toward a point where they can be more self-sufficient, and I can ride into the sunset....

At one point, during the late 1980s, Gerry says he did at least *consider* the possibility of selling the company's stock. "That was in the hey-day of the REITs [real estate investment trusts], when a lot of guys were selling their companies into REITs for tremendous multiples, all of which eventually went belly-up. But, anyway, some of our guys were talking about it at the time, so I finally said, 'O.K., let's go look at it.'

"I hired Arthur Andersen, the large auditing and consulting firm, as an advisor. We did all the paperwork, and then selected four of the big brokerage houses in New York, most of whom we knew because we'd done real estate projects with them in the past. We set up two days of meetings, morning and afternoon, each of the houses going through its presentation and a question-and-answer period. About halfway through the third one, one of the guys, who was one of the smartest people we knew on Wall Street, just stopped, looked at me, and said, 'Gerry, you're not going to sell this company, are you?' I suppose he could tell I was getting pretty tired of the meetings and hadn't been very enthused about the idea in the first place. So I said, 'No, I guess I'm not.' And, of course, we didn't. But it was good for our people to go through the informational process. After that, there was no more talk about going public."

To this day, the idea of the red tape and lack of control that he associates with public ownership obviously grates on Gerry. "When you're a public company, you're the servant of the servant of the servants," he says. "Thousands of people own your stock. And the inefficiencies are tremendous."

He says, while on the subject, that he learned a lot of valuable lessons serving on the board of the Peavey Company, the venerable Minneapolis-based milling and grain merchandising firm that, after more than a hundred years as a family-owned company, had gone public, then sold to ConAgra. "Frank Heffelfinger [a descendant of the original owners] told me, 'Gerry, we didn't sell the company now. We sold it when we went public.' That's something I think is important for everyone to remember. If you go public, you are selling the company. You're not just getting a chance to put a value on your stock—you're effectively selling it. If you want to keep the company in the family the way the Europeans do with their family businesses, you keep it private. You keep the business to yourself. You must avoid nepotism, of course. You have to find the best managers to run the firm, be they family or from outside the family, but you keep the stock to yourselves."

In 1991, Mark Rauenhorst remarked, "We expect our family business to go on forever." Later, he was quoted by Dave Beal in the *St. Paul Pioneer Press*, saying: "I don't feel family members have to be managers of the company. They just have to be involved in the governance of the company." In the same article, Gerry said, "Actually, I'd like to look to the twenty-second century. I'd like to leave a structure that makes that possible."

When Gerry first met Ned Bechtold, at a World Presidents Organization meeting in Buenos Aires in 1987, the conversation quickly centered on family and succession issues.

"We had a lot in common," Bechtold recalls. "We were both concerned about our family businesses. His was a first-generation family business, and mine was a second. We were both very concerned about the business continuing in the family. We didn't want to sell our companies, so succession planning was an important matter. It quickly became obvious that he was a man of vision, and that he was looking ahead to see how his business could continue on in the family after he was gone. People don't always want to think about that part of the business. Especially the founder of a company who might think he's going to live forever. But Gerry was clearly looking ahead."

As the friendship between the two men deepened, Bechtold met and was impressed by the Rauenhorst children. "I found them to be chips off the old block, all of them, serious and hard-working and great family people," he says. "They all had integrity—you could see it in their faces."

In the early 1990s, Bechtold (who joined the Opus board in 1993) continues, you could see a family company wrestling with inevitable change—"trying to find out what would work best when you have a second generation of seven children and only three of them are currently active in the business. How do you make that work and keep the family together? You could see things starting to take shape during that period, with the new leadership starting to emerge. Then it was interesting to see Gerry being involved and sort of indirectly directing it. Which is one of the interesting things about Gerry—he'll make things happen, yet make other people think they're doing it. Gerry will let people go for a while, and then he'll come up with ideas and make suggestions, and the others will say, 'Yeah, we didn't see it that way, but that makes sense....' He's a visionary, but he doesn't dream wild things. He sees things that are probably going to happen. Then he has the ability to get other people to share his vision and work in that direction. You don't see that very often, in a family business or in *any* business.

"And Gerry was very good about seeking outside counsel. He'd go to seminars and read books and talk to experts in the field of family business, and he'd listen to what his outside directors—some of whom, like myself and Susan Marvin [president of Marvin Windows and daughter of company founder William Marvin], were involved in family businesses and had similar concerns ourselves. He would ask advice and listen carefully and then fit things that made sense into the model he wanted to create for his situation.

"By the time I got involved, in the early nineties, he had a pretty good idea of where he wanted to go, but he was still always open to outside ideas. To a better way."

Opus board member Mike Sullivan says, "For at least the last quarter of a century, Gerry has been carefully putting into place a family company that he hopes will, after he's gone, not only survive but grow and prosper from one generation to the next and the next. That's not easy, but he's been at it for a long time, and I think there's a good chance it will happen."

Luz Campa, Gerry's old friend, colleague, and tax advisor, describes the Rauenhorst trust arrangement as the founder's "legacy to his offspring." He explains that Gerry arrived at this approach after studying European family businesses and observing how they survived and flourished from one generation to the next. Gerry views the business as a "family heirloom designed to exist in perpetuity," says Campa, who adds that the family's trusts were set up so that all of his heirs can benefit from that "heirloom." Campa underscores Gerry's belief that he has a moral obligation to give back as much as he's received. "He believes that God gave him his success for a purpose."

In April 1998, the family's second generation designated Keith Bednarowski and Luz Campa trustees of the two trusts that hold the company's common stock. The appointments were of critical importance, of course, but Campa nonetheless had to laugh. "Imagine that," he chuckled. "The kids of a German family picking a Polack and a Mexican as trustees!"

The Foundations

Peter Karoff, a Boston-based consultant who has worked with the Rauenhorsts on philanthropic concerns, jokes, "If anybody ever figures out how to take it with him, it will be Gerry!"

More seriously, Karoff says that Gerry's late-game focus has been on ensuring a viable family business *and* effective, ongoing philanthropy in the family's name. "He's a very tough-minded man, yet he remains open to outside ideas," Karoff says. "It's an interesting balance: strength and flexibility. But when he wants it to happen, he'll do whatever it takes."

Gerry's philanthropy rules, thought out and refined over several decades, include the following:

Don't invest in lost causes.

Don't make gifts just because you're friendly with the recipient.

Give to make the world a better place.

"We don't give gifts in order to enhance our personal standing in the community," he adds. "And most of our gifts are anonymous."

Recently, Don Neureuther, vice president of foundations, described the family's approach to multi-generational philanthropy. "I believe the real impact of the Rauenhorst family's generosity is yet to come," Neureuther, a former executive of the Oregon Community Foundation, who joined Opus in 2001, said. "And their generosity will continue long after Gerry and Hanky have left this earth."

"Each year—in good and not-so-good times—the Rauenhorsts have invested ten percent of Opus Corporation's pretax profits to support the charitable works of both the company and the family. That's an almost unheard of philanthropic investment in corporate America. This policy is supported not just by Gerry, but by his children and grandchildren, and has become one of the constants in how the family does business. That means that every year, with good stewardship, the assets of the foundations will most likely grow and the scope and impact of both family and company philanthropy will expand accordingly.

"When Gerry and Hanky established the family foundations—there are four of them in addition to the corporate foundation—they did so in an effort to challenge their family to develop more than one creative solution to address the pressing needs of the society in which the company operates. Day to day, that means that one foundation can function as an operating foundation, with family members becoming very involved in the programs they fund. Another foundation can be exclusively proactive in its grant-making, supporting just a few organizations each year in a substantial way. Another can be reactive, responding to the numerous requests for funding that the family receives.

"In January 2003, Gerry turned over the governance of the foundations to his seven children, their spouses, and some of the older members of the third generation. He considered that moment a watershed in the family's history—and who could disagree? Though not every member of the family has the skill set or interest to work in the family business, the foundation governance structure provides almost limitless opportunities for any and all family members to carry on Gerry and Hanky's legacy while establishing each succeeding generation's philanthropic traditions and history. It's worth noting that when Gerry was hiring me to help manage the foundations, he spoke passionately about the priority of ensuring his family's continued involvement in philanthropy.

"We're still in the early stages of 'professionalizing' the family's charitable giving," Neureuther continued. "We're still refining mission statements and strategic directions, and improving the daily conduct of the philanthropic 'business.' What the family, from Gerry and Hanky on down through the next two generations, has already clarified is their commitment to mirror in its philanthropic giving the sound business principles and values that have guided the company for the past fifty years. That translates into philanthropy that is entrepreneurial, proactive, focused, managed with integrity, and built on long-term relationships.

"We've got a lot of work ahead of us, and there's no guarantee that we will be successful—any more than Gerry and the Rauenhorst/Opus team were ever guaranteed of the business's success—but Gerry and Hanky have established a tradition that provides a valuable road map for the generations that will follow."

Third Generation and Beyond

On Saturday, May 3, 2003, Gerry Rauenhorst stood in front of 530 people—family members, friends, and Opus colleagues—to officially commemorate the fiftieth anniversary of the company's founding. More than 600 persons watched and listened via satellite feed simulcast to regional offices across four time zones. Significantly, Gerry was speaking from the atrium of Opus's largest construction project to date: the spectacular Best Buy campus in Richfield.

Tired from recent travel but clearly buoyed by the occasion, Gerry offered a pithy summation of his life and work, part of which follows:

> Walking into this room tonight and seeing the pictures of the fifties, sixties, seventies, eighties, and nineties...brought back many memories. Particularly of three families that span three-quarters of a century.
>
> The first was the family I grew up in, with six brothers and one sister. Our parents, especially our mother, had a profound influence on all of us. They taught us valuable lessons that shaped our lives and our careers. Those lessons—those core values—are the bedrock of the Opus culture today....
>
> Family values were indelibly impressed on us again and again. You don't lie. You don't cheat. Your reputation is everything. You stand up for what you believe in. That was the environment that pervaded the first of my families. The family of Henry and Margaret Rauenhorst in the twenties, thirties, and forties. It was an incredibly close-knit family that formed the values of the second family.
>
> That second family actually began with a homecoming dance in St. Paul.... I called a young lady from Bird Island.... She accepted. And I've never dated another lady since. We were married on September 2, 1950. Always since then, my beloved Hanky has been with me through thick and thin. She's been my inspiration....
>
> We were living in Wisconsin at the time I had my first taste of the construction business. It was a most unsatisfactory experience, working for that company. A second experience, in Minnesota, was the same.
>
> Then one evening, sitting at home with Hanky, I blurted out: "There has to be a better way." A way that is honest. And straight-forward. Where integrity counts. A way that emphasizes morality

and ethics. A way that rewards hard work. Where family values pervade the company.

So, on April 22, 1953—fifty years ago—we started Rauenhorst Construction Company. That's the date we signed our first contract—to build the Zion Lutheran Church in Olivia. I was employee number one. Hanky was employee number two.... I was contractor. Hanky was the chief financial officer....

My mother used to say, "Work hard and you'll succeed." And we did....

And now my third family. All 1,276 of you. You are the Opus family of today. You are the culmination of fifty years of hard work by many hundreds of people. You pattern your work lives on a Code of Conduct day in and day out, based on values that were formed in one generation and nurtured in the succeeding ones.

I have a dream for this family. I pray that the Opus of the year 2053—fifty years from now—will have ingrained in it the same strong values that moved through the Henry Rauenhorst family—and through the Gerald Rauenhorst family—to the Opus family of today. There are many reasons why Opus has been successful. I can tell you unequivocally that it all boils down to integrity. If Opus loses that, it will ultimately fail.

I hope that fifty years from now Opus will still have the entrepreneurial spirit it has today, pursuing new ideas and new ways of doing things, with determination. Emerson once wrote: "He is a well-made man who has good determination." Please God, let that continue to characterize the leadership of this corporation—long after I'm gone—when Opus celebrates its one hundredth anniversary.

In the meantime, let me assure all of you that I am most comfortable with our direction and our leadership. Opus is in a very strong position under two very capable executives—Mark Rauenhorst, our CEO, and Keith Bednarowski, our chairman. They are men of integrity and vision. Together they have fifty-six years of experience with Opus. They understand its strengths and its weaknesses. They know its capabilities. They fully embrace its culture and its core values.

As I ride off into the sunset, I know this company is in very, very good hands, and I am very satisfied and content.

Gerry paused for a moment. Then, a master of timing, he added:

I don't know where I'll be fifty years from now, but let me assure you, wherever I am, I'll be watching.

Timeline

The following is a chronology of important events in the Gerald A. Rauenhorst family and the Opus Group of Companies through 2003. Also included are some of the 2,100 Opus construction projects the company has completed since its founding in 1953.

1842

- Theodore Rauenhorst, Gerry's grandfather, is born in Westphalia,

1880

- Theodore's son, Henry Theodore, is born in Easton, Minnesota.

1900

- Twenty-year-old Henry Theodore Rauenhorst makes his way to Renville County, Minnesota, to homestead a 240-acre farm between Bird Island and Olivia.

1908

- Henry Theodore marries Margaret Keltgen, a neighbor whose family had emigrated from Luxembourg during the late 1880s.

1925

- Hard-working and ambitious, Henry and Margaret own three farms in Renville County. But, following exorbitant assessments on their land, they lose their farms and are forced to become tenant farmers on rented land north of Bird Island.

1927

- Gerald Anthony, the seventh of Henry and Margaret's eight children, is born at the University of Minnesota Hospital in Minneapolis.
- Henrietta Schmoll is born. She is the youngest of three daughters of Henry and Sophia Schmoll, who farm not far from the Henry Rauenhorsts in Renville County.

1930

- Eager for opportunities during the first few years of the Great Depression, Henry Rauenhorst's family agrees to take part in a project developed by the University of Minnesota to develop a more productive hybrid seed corn. The business eventually develops into the Trojan Seed Company.

1933

- Gerry, age five, and his younger brother, Bob, launch their first business venture, selling sweet corn from the family's field at a small stand they built on a nearby highway.
- Gerry is enrolled in the first grade at St. Aloysius Catholic School in Olivia.
- Henrietta Schmoll, meanwhile, attends a county school south of Bird Island.

1935

- The Rauenhorsts plant almost a thousand acres of sweet corn under contract with a local canning company.

1937

- Ten-year-old Gerry is enlisted by his brother George to help set up a mink-farming operation on the family property. The project, which teaches the boys several difficult lessons, is abandoned a year later.

1940

- The Rauenhorst family begins raising turkeys, selling them to Swift and Company and making enough money to cover their investment. Gerry is put in charge of the operation, and the business continues for several years.
- Gerry begins public high school in Olivia.
- Henrietta attends St. Mary's Catholic High School in Bird Island.

1941

- The family's hybrid seed-corn enterprise continues to grow, with sales to Cargill and Northrup King. By the early 1940s, the family is working about 2,000 acres of rented land.

1944

- Gerry completes his first off-the-farm construction project with brother Bob: a thousand-seat concrete-block and wooden-plank "stadium" for Olivia's semi-pro baseball team. Holding sole rights to the concessions, the boys cover their costs and pay off their loans in two years.
- Henrietta graduates from high school.

1945

- Gerry graduates from high school and enrolls at the College of St. Thomas in St. Paul, Minnesota, beginning a three-year accelerated program with a focus in economics.

1946

- To help cover his college expenses, Gerry sells encyclopedias door-to-door. The second week on the job he earns $65.
- Henrietta enrolls at the College of St. Catherine in St. Paul and begins working toward a degree in home economics.

1947

- Gerry asks Henrietta to be his date for Tiger Homecoming at St. Thomas. She accepts, and, from that day on, he never dates anyone else.
- Gerry coins the nickname Hanky, which Henrietta will be called the rest of her life.

1948

- Gerry graduates from St. Thomas in the spring and in the fall is admitted into the engineering program at Marquette University in Milwaukee.

1949

- Hanky graduates from St. Catherine and accepts a position as a home economist with Northern States Power Company in Minneapolis.
- Gerry learns to fly, buys a $500 airplane, and maintains his long-distance courtship of Hanky with frequent flights between Milwaukee and the Twin Cities.

1950

- Gerry accepts a full-time job, at $3,120 a year, as an engineering instructor while finishing his classes at Marquette.
- Hanky secures a home economics job at the Wisconsin Gas Company in Milwaukee.
- Hanky and Gerry are married at St. Mary's Catholic Church in Bird Island. After honeymooning in the Canadian Rockies, they set up housekeeping in a Milwaukee apartment.

1951

- In March, Gerry graduates from Marquette with a degree in civil engineering. In August, he lands his first job, earning $80 a week, handling the bidding process for a small contractor in Wisconsin.
- In December, the Rauenhorsts' first child, Judith, is born.

1952

- Dissatisfied with his job in Wisconsin, Gerry and his family return to Minnesota, where he takes an estimator's job with a construction company at a salary of $100 a week.
- Later in the year, Gerry explores the possibility of starting his own company, and the family moves into its first home, a small bungalow in Richfield, Minnesota, a Minneapolis suburb.

1953

- The Rauenhorsts' second child, Mark, is born in February.
- In April, Gerry goes into business for himself, working out of a breezeway "office" in his Richfield home and calling his enterprise Trojan Construction.
- The company's first project is the $56,000 Zion Lutheran Church in Olivia.

Other projects this year include:
- *Trojan Seed Company, Olivia, MN*
- *University of Minnesota, Rosemount, MN*
- *Mutual Creamery Insurance Company, Richfield, MN*

1954

- Gerry changes the company's name to Rauenhorst Construction to avoid confusion with the family's seed-corn business in Olivia.
- Son Neil is born.

Projects include:
- *Church of Seven Dolors Convent, Albany, MN*
- *St. Peter's Catholic Church addition, Richfield, MN*
- *Pure Oil truck stop, Olivia, MN*

1955

- Gerry builds the company's second (the first freestanding) headquarters, at 7848 Fremont Avenue in Bloomington, Minnesota.

Projects include:
- *National Farm Loan Association, Redwood Falls, MN*
- *St. Ambrose Church and Rectory, St. Paul, MN*
- *Farmers' Home Mutual Insurance, Minneapolis, MN*

1956

• Son Joseph is born.

Projects include:

  • *St. Andrew's School, St. Paul, MN*
  • *Nelson Elementary School, Columbia Heights, MN*
  • *Cooper and Tilden Schools, Hastings, MN*

1957

• Son Michael is born.
• By year's end, Rauenhorst Construction has completed more than fifty buildings in Minnesota.

Projects include:

  • *Interstate G.M. Diesel, Bloomington, MN*
  • *St. Patrick's Episcopal Church, Bloomington, MN*
  • *Luger Boats, Bloomington, MN*
  • *Glenmar Building, Bloomington, MN*

1958

• Gerry, Hanky, and their five children move to a larger home in Edina, another Minneapolis suburb.
• The company lands its first major project: Dowling residence hall on the St. Paul campus of the University of St. Thomas.

Other projects include:

  • *Pacific Toy House, Bloomington, MN*
  • *Products Design & Engineering, Golden Valley, MN*
  • *Rosemount Engineering, Bloomington, MN*

1959

- Rauenhorst Construction builds its third headquarters — at 5000 West 78th Street in Bloomington — to accommodate the needs of a rapidly growing company.

Projects include:
- *Research Engineering, Eden Prairie, MN*
- *Lowell Inn, Stillwater, MN*
- *College of St. Catherine, St. Paul, MN*

1960

- Gerry joins the board of the Bloomington-Richfield branch of Northwestern Bank.

Projects include:
- *Wonderly Building, Bloomington, MN*
- *20th Century Manufacturing, Bloomington, MN*
- *Nazareth Hall Day School, St. Paul, MN*

1961

- Gerry decides his company should become a turnkey — or design/build — operation that will revolutionize the industry. An early turnkey project is an office and manufacturing facility designed and built for the Toro Company in Bloomington.
- Rauenhorst Construction begins to develop Normandale Industrial Park in Edina and Bloomington, Minnesota.

Projects include:
- *Control Data Corporation, Bloomington, MN*
- *Chancery Residence, St. Paul, MN*
- *Normandale Golf Course, Edina, MN*

1962

• Daughter Susan is born.

Projects include:

- *Xerox Corporation, Richfield, MN*
- *Dunn & Curry Office Building, Edina, MN*
- *Federal Tool and Manufacturing, Bloomington, MN*

1963

• In Richfield, Rauenhorst Construction completes the first Howard Johnson Motor Lodge built west of the Mississippi. The company will eventually build four more HoJo's.

• Rauenhorst Construction moves into its fourth headquarters — at 4444 Rauenhorst Circle in Bloomington.

• At the end of its first decade, the company has an annual construction volume of $6.5 million and about 175 employees. The company has completed more than 210 projects.

Other projects include:

- *Research, Inc., Eden Prairie, MN*
- *M.A.Gedney Company, Chaska, MN*
- *Peterson Seed Company, Savage, MN*

1964

• Daughter Amy is born.

• Gerry and Hanky visit Christ Church College at Oxford University in England, where Gerry envisions how a modern, urban university campus in the Twin Cities might look.

Projects include:

- *R.C. Hitchcock & Sons, Bloomington, MN*
- *United Mailing Corporation, Edina, MN*
- *Camelot Restaurant, Bloomington, MN*

1965

• Gerry changes the company's name from Rauenhorst Construction to Rauenhorst Corporation.

Projects include:

- *Hazelden Foundation, Center City, MN*
- *Farm Bureau Office Building, Woodbury, MN*
- *Pentagon Office Tower, Edina, MN*
- *Precision Circuits Corporation, Bloomington, MN*
- *Normandale Veterinary Hospital, Bloomington, MN*

1966

• The Rauenhorsts' eighth child, Gerald Anthony, dies at six weeks.

• Gerry is elected to the board of trustees of the College of St. Thomas, where he serves to this day.

• Rauenhorst Corporation adopts its familiar dark blue hexagonal logo.

Projects include:

- *State Farm Insurance, Edina, MN*
- *Pillsbury Company Warehouse, Golden Valley, MN*
- *Donaldson Company, Bloomington, MN*

1967

Projects include:

- *United Warehouse, Plymouth, MN*
- *Business Incentives, Minneapolis, MN*
- *Minnesota Twins/Metropolitan Stadium addition, Bloomington, MN*
- *Northwestern Bell Telephone, Brooklyn Center, MN*
- *Old Dutch Foods, Roseville, MN*
- *Pillsbury Company, Peoria, IL*
- *Lakeside Industries, Bloomington, MN*

1968

Projects include:

- *APA Food Services, Inc., Bloomington, MN*
- *Archer Daniels Midland, Decatur, IL*
- *Coca-Cola Bottling, Eagan, MN*
- *Control Data Corporation, Minneapolis, MN*

1969

- Gerry is named Marquette University's Alumnus of the Year, the youngest honoree in the twenty-five-year history of the award.
- Pentagon Park, covering more than sixty acres and containing twenty-one Rauenhorst-built buildings, is completed in Edina and Bloomington, Minnesota.
- Keith Bednarowski joins the company as a project manager.

Projects include:

- *American Motors Company, Bloomington, MN*
- *Menasha Corporation, Minneapolis, MN*
- *Employers Mutual of Wausau, Edina, MN*
- *Data 100 Corporation, Edina, MN*
- *Gould, Inc., Mendota Heights, MN*

1970

- Gerry joins the Norwest Bank Corporation board.
- He adds the first outsider to the Rauenhorst Corporation board: Clarence Frame, CEO of the First National Bank of St. Paul.
- Gerry is elected to Marquette University's board of trustees, on which he will serve for thirty years.

Projects include:

- *Chicago Tube & Iron, Eagan, MN*
- *Red Owl Stores, Eagan, MN*
- *State Farm Insurance, Fridley, MN*
- *Minnesota Mining & Manufacturing Company (3M), St. Paul, MN*

1971

- The company's Fabcon subsidiary is founded to manufacture hollow-core panels for walls, floors, and ceilings.
- The company develops the 1/40 Program, committing one executive hour out of every forty and $1 out of every $40 of earnings to a separate non-profit corporation that funds Progress Valley, Inc., which provides continuing care and motivation to persons recovering from chemical addiction.

Projects include:
- *J.C. Penney Company, Edina, MN*
- *St. Paul Union Stockyards, St. Paul, MN*
- *Northwestern Bell Telephone, Maplewood, MN*

1972

- Keith Bednarowski opens a Rauenhorst Corporation office in Milwaukee, Wisconsin.

Projects include:
- *Farm House Foods, Eau Claire, WI*
- *Reynolds Metals, St. Louis Park, MN*
- *Northwestern College, St. Paul, MN*
- *Creamette Corporation, New Hope, MN*
- *Northwestern Financial Center, Bloomington, MN*

1973

- Rauenhorst Corporation celebrates its twentieth anniversary and breaks ground for the Opus 2 development on more than 300 acres of erstwhile farmland in Minnetonka, a southwestern suburb of Minneapolis.
- Gerry stresses the importance of ethics in a commencement address at the University of St. Thomas, where he receives an honorary Doctor of Laws degree.

Projects include:
- *Data 100 Corporation (in Opus 2), Minnetonka, MN*
- *Northern States Power Company, Sioux Falls, SD*
- *Graco addition, Minneapolis, MN*
- *Graybar Electric, Sioux Falls, SD*
- *AgChem, Jackson, MN*
- *Marquette University athletic facility, Milwaukee, WI*

1974

- The company moves its headquarters into the twenty-second and twenty-third floors of the Rauenhorst-built Northwestern Financial Center, its fifth headquarters in twenty-one years.
- Gerry commissions McKinsey & Company, a national consulting firm, to study the business as it enters its third decade. Rauenhorst Corporation subsequently reorganizes into two divisions.
- Luz Campa joins the company.

Projects include:
- *Tennant Company, Maple Grove, MN*
- *Georgia Pacific, Maple Grove, MN*
- *Hazelden Foundation, Center City, MN*
- *McKesson & Robbins (Acryltech Building), Little Canada, MN*
- *Armour & Company, Cold Spring, MN*
- *Valleyfair Amusement Park, Shakopee, MN*

1975

- Gerry, Hanky, and their seven children move into a new home that Gerry built in Edina.
- John Albers joins the company.

Projects include:
- *Jamestown Shopping Center, Jamestown, ND*
- *Coast to Coast Stores, Crawfordsville, IN*
- *American State Bank of Olivia, Olivia, MN*
- *Target Stores, Minneapolis, MN*
- *Kraft Foods, Plymouth, MN*

1976
Projects include:

- *Opportunity Workshop, Minnetonka, MN*
- *Fisher Scientific, Itaska, IL*
- *Totino's Fine Foods, Fridley, MN*
- *Briggs & Stratton, Milwaukee, WI*
- *Arctic Cat, Plymouth, MN*

1977
Projects include:

- *Allis Chalmers Company, Appleton, WI*
- *West Publishing, Eagan, MN*
- *Outboard Marine Corporation, Morrow, GA*
- *Data Card Corporation, Minnetonka, MN*

1978

- A private plane crash near Kenyon, Minnesota, kills Gerry's brother Bob, two nephews, and three others.
- Gerry receives the Distinguished Alumnus Award from the College of St. Thomas Alumni Association, its highest award.
- At its twenty-fifth anniversary, the company has logged more than 670 projects, totaling more than $400 million, in twelve states. The company has sales of $91.7 million.

Projects include:

- *American Family Insurance, St. Joseph, MO*
- *Signode Corporation, Itaska, IL*
- *Munsingwear, Ironwood, MI*
- *Ben Franklin Stores Warehouse, Seymour, IN*
- *Target Stores, Sioux Falls, SD*

1979

- Rauenhorst Corporation surpasses the $100 million sales mark.
- A new office is opened in Chicago, Illinois.

Projects include:

- *Brown & Bigelow, St. Paul, MN*
- *Continental Can, Downers Grove, IL*
- *National Car Rental, Edina, MN*
- *Burlington-Northern, Alliance, NE*
- *Miller Brewing, Wauwatosa, WI*
- *Southwest Financial Center, Phoenix, AZ*
- *Kensington Center for Business, Mount Prospect, IL*

1980

- A new office opens in Phoenix, Arizona, becomes headquarters for the Opus West region.
- Hanky is elected a trustee of the College of St. Catherine.

Projects include:

- *Deluxe Check Printers, Bensonville, IL*
- *Broadway Business Center, Minneapolis, MN*
- *Opus Center, Minnetonka, MN*

1981

Projects include:

- *Phelps Dodge, Phoenix, AZ*
- *Wisconsin Bell Telephone, West Allis, WI*
- *IBM Office Building, Sioux Falls, SD*
- *Minnesota Mutual Fire & Casualty, Minnetonka, MN*

1982

- Dyson & Company is purchased in Pensacola, Florida.
- Gerry is elected to the board of ConAgra.
- Mark Rauenhorst, after several positions with other corporations, joins the family business in Minnetonka. Neil Rauenhorst, after a three-year stint with a prestigious architectural firm, joins the company in Chicago. Judy Rauenhorst Mahoney joins the company's marketing department after working in communications in both industry and state government.
- The company moves into its sixth headquarters—at 9900 Bren Road East, Minnetonka.
- The company formally changes its name to Opus Corporation. Opus is Latin for "creative work."

Projects include:
- *Hartzell Corporation, St. Paul, MN*
- *Ventura Plaza, Scottsdale, AZ*
- *Associated Grocers, Denver, CO*

1983

- Dyson & Company expands to Tampa, Florida.
- *Corporate Report Minnesota* magazine names Gerry its Executive of the Year.
- The *Congressional Record* publishes Gerry's advocacy of educational deregulation.
- Opus builds for the first time in downtown Minneapolis: a twenty-three-floor office tower known by its address, 100 South Fifth Street.

Other projects include:
- *American Hotel Register Company, Northbrook, IL*
- *Norwest Bank, Bloomington, MN*
- *3M, DeKalb, IL*

1984

- Celebrating thirty years in business, Opus manages seventy-four projects containing seven million square feet in a dozen metropolitan areas; the company owns all or a part of the projects.
- The Rauenhorst family begins its formal twice-a-year business meetings.

Projects include:

- *Northwestern Mutual Life Insurance, Eagan, MN*
- *Porsche facility, Reno, NV*
- *Eastman Kodak, Mount Prospect, IL*
- *Westshore Place, Tampa, FL*

1985

Projects include:

- *Northwestern Publishing, Wauwatosa, WI*
- *Boise Cascade, Brooklyn Park, MN*
- *Hilton Hotel (Minneapolis–St. Paul International Airport), Bloomington, MN*

1986

Projects include:

- *150 South Fifth Street, Minneapolis, MN*
- *Federal Express, Wauwatosa, WI*
- *St. Therese Care Center, Hopkins, MN*
- *Honda facility, Glendale, WI*

1987

Projects include:

- *Black & Decker Service Center, Wauwatosa, WI*
- *Raytheon Corporation, Addison, IL*
- *Kraft Foods, Cincinnati, OH*
- *American Hardware Mutual, Minnetonka, MN*

1988

- Neil Rauenhorst becomes president of Opus South in Tampa, Florida.
- Gerry and four other American lay Catholics begin to organize and raise an endowment available for the Pope's use at his discretion.
- The company forms its Opus North region, with headquarters in Chicago.

Projects include:

- *ConAgra–Frozen IOC, Omaha, NE*
- *National Computer Systems, Eagan, MN*
- *Marriott Hotel, Minnetonka, MN*
- *Kraft Foodservice Group, Cincinnati, OH*

1989

- Joe Rauenhorst joins Opus after practicing law in San Francisco for eight years. He later becomes president of the Opus South region.
- Hanky completes her term as a St. Catherine trustee and becomes trustee emerita; for the next five years she will serve as honorary chairwoman of the college's capital campaign.

Projects include:

- *Rosemount Engineering, Chanhassen, MN*
- *First Bank Place, Minneapolis, MN*
- *Cold Springs Center, St. Cloud, MN*
- *West Publishing Computer Center, Eagan, MN*

1990

- Opus builds a thirty-five-acre campus for ConAgra that revitalizes the core of downtown Omaha. The campus comprises 600,000 square feet in five buildings designed by John Albers, president of Opus architects and engineers, reminiscent of the Prairie School style of Frank Lloyd Wright.
- Gerry is appointed to the board of the Ninth Federal Reserve District.

Projects include:
- *Allen Bradley Company, Mequon, WI*
- *State of Washington Labor and Industry Building, Tumwater, WA*
- *Dayton's Distribution Center, St. Paul, MN*
- *Schneider (USA), Plymouth, MN*

1991

- Keith Bednarowski becomes CEO and president of Opus.
- Opus publishes a formal Code of Conduct to which every director, officer, and employee must subscribe.

Projects include:
- *U.S. Postal Service D.D.C., Kent, WA*
- *American Medical Systems, Minnetonka, MN*
- *Clark Printing Company, Liberty, MO*

1992

- Opus is honored as National Developer of the Year by the National Association of Industrial and Office Properties.
- Opus completes the first building of a downtown Minneapolis campus for the University of St. Thomas.
- For his "incontrovertible loyalty to the Catholic Church," Gerry is made a Knight of the Order of St. Gregory, the highest honor the Vatican can bestow on a lay person.

Projects include:
- *University of Minnesota (Mariucci Arena), Minneapolis, MN*
- *Banta ISG Bushman Press, Spanish Fork, UT*

1993
- Opus celebrates its fortieth anniversary.
- Ned Bechtold, CEO of Payne and Dolan in Waukesha, Wisconsin, joins the Opus board.

Projects include:
  - *International Dairy Queen, Edina, MN*
  - *State Office Building, Sacramento, CA*
  - *American Furniture Warehouse, Thornton, CO*
  - *Enterprise Building, Omaha, NE*

1994
- The company forms the Opus East region, with headquarters in Washington, D.C.
- Mike Sullivan, CEO of International Dairy Queen, joins the Opus board.
- The Opus Northwest region is formed, with headquarters in Minnetonka.

Projects include:
  - *Tulsa Retail/Media Play, Tulsa, OK*
  - *Payless Cashways, Las Vegas, NV*

1995
- *National Real Estate Investor* magazine names Opus the nation's number-one developer.
- Gerry completes his term as chairman of the Ninth Federal Reserve Board.

Projects include:
  - *Maplewood Park Place, Bethesda, MD*
  - *Waldorf Corporation, Maple Grove, MN*

1996

Projects include:

- *Eagan Promenade, Eagan, MN*
- *Polaris Industries, Vermillion, SD*
- *U.S. West Office Building, Maple Grove, MN*

1997

Projects include:

- *Field Paper Company, Ankeny, IA*
- *Alliance Data, Northglenn, CO*
- *National Computer Systems, Cedar Rapids, IA*
- *PacifiCare Health Systems, Englewood, CO*

1998

- Opus moves to its current corporate headquarters, at 10350 Bren Road West in Opus 2.
- Susan Marvin, president of Marvin Windows, joins the Opus board.
- Keith Bednarowski and Luz Campa are selected by the Rauenhorst children to be trustees of the two trusts that hold the company's common stock.

Projects include:

- *Sammamish Park Place, Issaquah, WA*
- *Southcreek Corporation Campus, Overland Park, KS*
- *Pulte Homes, Englewood, CO*

1999

- Mark Rauenhorst becomes president of Opus.

Projects include:

- *Arbor Lakes Retail, Maple Grove, MN*
- *St. Ambrose of Woodbury, Woodbury, MN*
- *Blake Street Offices, Denver, CO*

2000

- Opus forms Encore One to acquire companies with business cycles that complement Opus's cycles.
- Mark Rauenhorst is named president and CEO of Opus, Keith Bednarowski, chairman, and Gerry, founding chairman.
- Annual revenues reach $1.4 billion.
- Gerry and Hanky celebrate their fiftieth wedding anniversary with the entire family in France.

Projects include:

- *American Express Financial Advisors, Minneapolis, MN*
- *Eastpointe Corporate Center, Issaquah, WA*
- *Benilde–St. Margaret's School, St. Louis Park, MN*
- *The Crossings, Allentown, PA*

2001

- After thirty years in operation, Progress Valley programs in the Twin Cities and Phoenix have graduated more than 6,000 persons.
- Ground is broken on a 3.6-million-square-foot campus in suburban Minneapolis for Best Buy Corporation, the largest project in Opus's nearly fifty-year history.
- Marquette University grants Gerry an honorary Doctor of Laws degree.

Projects include:

- *Airport 100 buildings, Hanover, MD*
- *Luther College Center for the Arts, Decorah, IA*
- *U.S. Bank, St. Paul, MN*
- *University of St. Thomas School of Law, Minneapolis, MN*

2002

- Encore One makes its first acquisition, Marsden, a Minneapolis-based company in the security, money transfer, and building-cleaning businesses.
- Neil Rauenhorst leaves Opus to open his own development company in Tampa, Florida.
- A master plan for a corporate campus to be built by Opus for Northwestern Mutual in suburban Milwaukee, Wisconsin, is announced.

Projects include:
- *Alliant Energy World Headquarters, Madison, WI*
- *College of St. Catherine Student Center, St. Paul, MN*
- *Marvin Home Center, Warroad, MN*
- *Camelback Esplanade V, Phoenix, AZ*

2003

- Opus is fifty years old, with 1,276 employees (including 90 architects and engineers) and offices in five regions and twenty-seven locations. It has completed more than 2,100 buildings from coast to coast.
- Gerry transfers governance of the foundations to his seven children, their spouses, and some of the older members of the family's third generation.
- On May 3, in a Twin Cities program simulcast to the company's five regions, Gerry formally announces his retirement. He says, "I don't know where I'll be fifty years from now, but let me assure you that wherever I am, I will be watching."

Projects include:
- *GSA FDOT Office Building, Lakewood, CO*
- *Oneida Cold Storage and Warehouse, Henderson, CO*
- *Marquette University (Al McGuire Center), Milwaukee, WI*
- *Sancerre Luxury Condominiums, Naples, FL*

Acknowledgments

This book, like the buildings it describes, is not the work of a single individual, but instead the result of the combined and coordinated efforts of many. All who contributed a "voice" — family members, friends, colleagues, journalists, and other observers — are acknowledged in the text. To each and everyone of you who had something kind to say, I say thank you.

There are a few individuals, however, who have been more directly and extensively involved in the conception, planning, and construction of *A Better Way*, and to each of them I want to give special thanks.

My dear friend Monsignor Terrence Murphy was an enthusiastic supporter of the project from the beginning and wrote, at my request, the book's gracious foreword. Keith Bednarowski and Luz Campa, Opus's chairman and longtime tax authority, respectively, and both among my most trusted advisors, gave the text careful readings and constructive criticism. Don Neureuther, who oversees our foundations and philanthropic work, did the same, adding the perspective of someone somewhat newer to the Opus/Rauenhorst family. Carol Blanchard, my executive assistant in Florida, handled much of the tedious production work, and Judy Truex, my executive assistant in Minnesota, tended to the essential fine points from start to finish, and has been, as she's been with all manner of projects during the past twenty-five years, indispensable. William Swanson reviewed, compiled, and edited three-quarters of a century of family lore and fifty years of corporate accounts, then connected the dots, filled in the blanks, and made the whole thing cohesive and readable. Joan Henrik, art director at the Westmorelandflint advertising, marketing, and public relations firm in Duluth, designed the book inside and out.

Finally, there's my old friend and counselor Quentin J. Hietpas, without whom this book, quite honestly, wouldn't exist. It was Quent who encouraged the idea of a family and corporate history, brought Bill and Joan into the mix, and spent countless hours during the past two years making sure everything and everyone stayed on track. If there ever was an invaluable project superintendent, believe me, it was Quent.

My gratitude for the imagination, resourcefulness, and hard work you all brought to this book exceeds my ability to express it.

G.A.R.

Index

A

Aetna Life, 160, 161

AgChem, 237

Airport 100 buildings, 246

Albany, Minnesota, 47

Albers, John W., *116*, 159, 165, 176, 181, 183, 237, 242

Allen Bradley Company, 243

Allen Edmunds Corporation, 128

Alliance Data, 245

Alliant Energy World Headquarters, 247

Allis Chalmers Company, 238

Alumnus of the Year (Marquette University), 146, 154, 235

American Express Financial Advisors, 201, 246

American Family Insurance, 160, 238

American Furniture Warehouse, 244

American Hardware Mutual, 241

American Hotel Register Company, 240

American Linen Supply, 164

American Medical Systems, 243

American Motors Company, 235

American State Bank, Olivia, 158, 237

Annex, The, 29

Annunciation Church, Minneapolis, 55

Apache Corporation, 163

APA Food Services, Inc., 235

Aquinas, Thomas, 31

Arbor Lakes Retail, 245

Archer Daniels Midland, 235

Architecture Minnesota, 165

Arctic Cat, 238

Armour & Company, 237

Arthur Andersen, 215

Ascent, 175

Associated Grocers, 240

Atlanta, Georgia, 194

Augustine, Saint, 89

B

Bakken, Earl, 13

Bank of America, 191

Banta ISG Bushman Press, 243

Baumgartner, Muriel Rauenhorst, 19, 23, 28, *99*, *127*

Beal, Dave, 174, 216

Bechtold, Ned, 93, 146, 210, 216-217, 244

Bednarowski, Keith, 83-84, 85, *132*, 153, 163, 166, 175, 176, 184, 186, 197, 198, 218, 222, 235, 236, 243, 245, 246, 249

Ben Franklin Stores Warehouse, 238

Benilde-St. Margaret's School, 246

Benjamin Thompson & Associates, 161

Berkshire Hathaway Inc., *121*, 154

Photo captions are indicated in bold face, italic type.